# JAMES DEAN

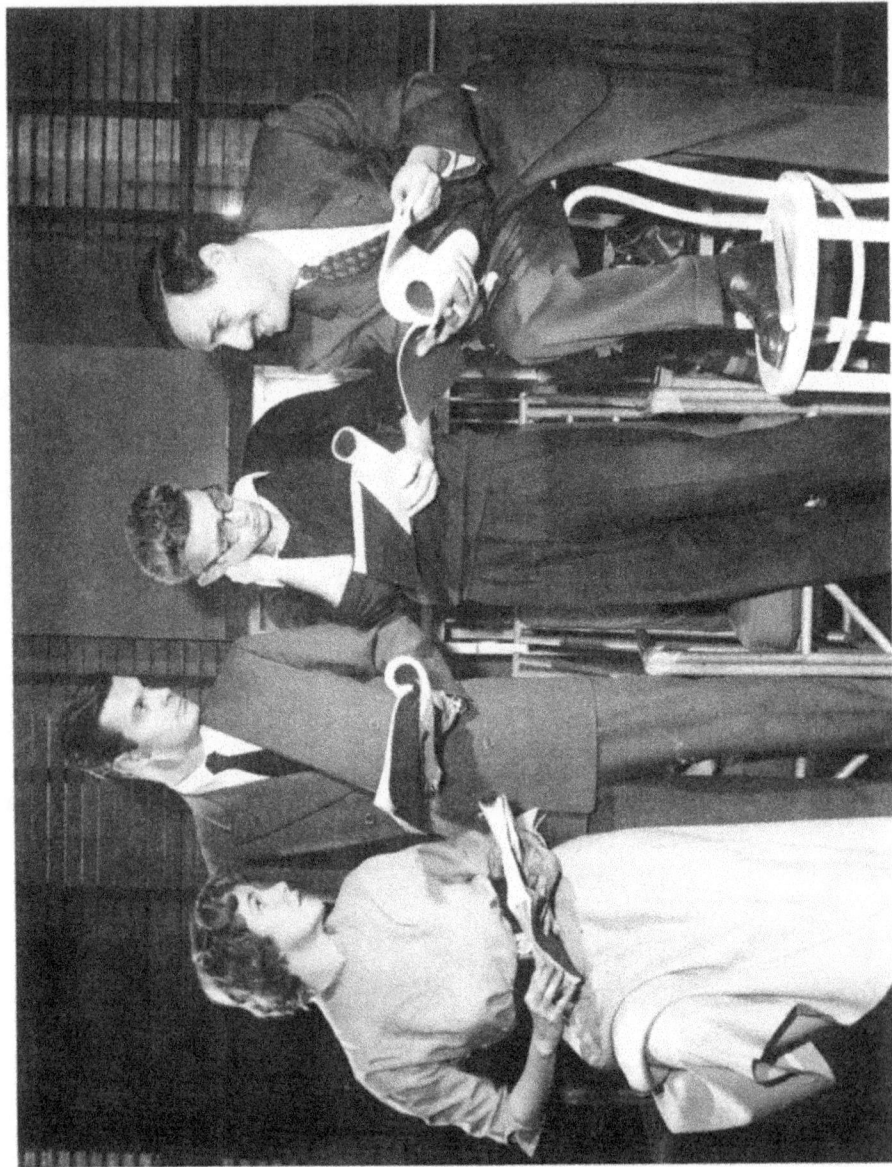

Geraldine Page, Louis Jourdan, James Dean, and Donald Stewart reading for *The Immoralist*. (Photograph courtesy of Photofest)

# JAMES DEAN

## A Bio-Bibliography

### David Hofstede

Bio-Bibliographies in the Performing Arts, Number 71
*James Robert Parish, Series Adviser*

GREENWOOD PRESS
Westport, Connecticut • London

**Library of Congress Cataloging-in-Publication Data**

Hofstede, David.
   James Dean : a bio-bibliography / David Hofstede.
     p.  cm.—(Bio-bibliographies in the performing arts, ISSN
0892–5550 ; no. 71)
   Discography: p.
   Filmography: p.
   Includes bibliographical references and index.
   ISBN 0–313–29475–5 (alk. paper)
   1. Dean, James, 1931–1955.  2. Dean, James, 1931–1955—
Bibliography.  3. Motion picture actors and actresses—United
States—Biography.  I. Title.  II. Series.
PN2287.D33H53  1996
791.43′028′092—dc20
  [B]       95–46112

British Library Cataloguing in Publication Data is available.

Library of Congress Catalog Card Number: 95–46112
ISBN: 0–313–29475–5
ISSN: 0892–5550

First published in 1996

Greenwood Press, 88 Post Road West, Westport, CT 06881
An imprint of Greenwood Publishing Group, Inc.

Printed in the United States of America

∞™

The paper used in this book complies with the
Permanent Paper Standard issued by the National
Information Standards Organization (Z39.48–1984).

10 9 8 7 6 5 4 3 2 1

For the Deaners, who keep the legend alive.

# CONTENTS

# ILLUSTRATIONS

# PREFACE

*James Dean: A Bio-Bibliography* joins over 25 biographies and hundreds of magazine articles about James Dean that have already been published. I began my research with the full realization that, in the 30 years since his death at the age of 24, a wealth of extraordinary documentation of Dean's life and career is available, and it is doubtful that any more major revelations will ever surface. My goal was not to break any new ground, but to assemble as much of the information that is both available and accurate, into one user-friendly, objective volume.

Every trivial bit of minutiae concerning Dean's life, Dean's career and Dean's death is written down somewhere. In less than 30 days, I had discovered that Dean's social security number was 310-28-1959, and that Collier Davidson was the ambulance attendant who arrived on the scene of the fatal accident on September 30, 1955, a date that is as well-known to Dean's legion of fans as the date of their birth. What is more difficult to find, particularly for the researcher or film historian, is non-biased coverage of the man behind the icon, and impartial assessment of his achievements in a far too brief career.

"Tell-alls," and "exposes" have become a cottage industry and compose the most unpleasant facet of the enduring Dean phenomenon. Almost everyone who ever met James Dean is under contract, and will not speak about their friendship/romance/working relationship without compensation. Most have written their own articles or books, and there is no question that a sizable readership awaits any addition to the canon. Still feeling cheated at having just three major movies in which to cheer their idol, the Dean faithful devour every new take on old, familiar subjects, regardless of accuracy.

Most James Dean biographies contain the same quotes, the same anecdotes, and a deep, abiding respect for an immensely talented actor. They also share a profound sorrow at the loss of one so gifted before the age of 30. No one in the century-old history of motion pictures ever left with more unrealized potential. However dubiously one might view the strange Dean death-cult, there was undeniably in Dean something genuine to get excited about.

Where the existing material deviates is in the coverage of Dean's shortcomings, of which there were many. While the tabloid accounts predictably exaggerate, and sometimes outright fabricate, lurid accounts of Dean's sexual behavior and slovenly personal habits, the more legitimate biographies are often guilty of favoring the opposite extreme. If the less appealing characteristics of James Dean are acknowledged, they are seldom, if ever, condemned. The derogatory comments of Rock Hudson regarding Dean's comportment on the set of *Giant*, for example, are usually reported and then presented in the guise of a lightweight movie star who was jealous of a "real" actor. Friends of James Dean tolerated his ferocious temper, his brooding, his selfishness, and his quixotic mood swings, often just for the opportunity of remaining a part of his "inner circle."

What may be the most fascinating aspect of Dean's career is his attitude toward his work. He would emanate disdain for a job after he was hired, but inside he was thrilled just to be a part of show business. The "method" actor, the serious artiste that was James Dean, could be as starstruck himself as the thirteen-year-old girls who tacked his picture to their bedroom doors. One of Dean's proudest moments on the set of *Rebel Without a Cause* was learning how to imitate Mr. Magoo from costar Jim Backus, though such silly pleasures seem incongruous with the brooding rebel image that is now permanently attached to his name.

His performances were lauded for a depth of emotion he could convincingly summon in character, but that he could never show when the camera stopped. This, perhaps, is the greatest irony of James Dean as an actor, and as a man.

*James Dean: A Bio-Bibliography* is divided into eleven sections:

1.     A short biography.

2.     A chronology of important events in his career and personal life.

3.     A list of his stage appearances, including college plays and summer stock.

4.     A filmography, including complete cast and credits for each film plus a synopsis, review summary, and commentary.

5.     Appearances in radio, television dramas, and commercials.

6.     A discography of song and related recordings.

7.      An annotated bibliography of magazine articles, newspaper
        articles, and books about Dean or referring to him.

8.      A list of awards won by Dean.

9.      A list of movie roles offered to Dean during his career, and of
        roles he might have played.

10.     A list of stage, film, and recording tributes to James Dean.

11.     A complete index of names and titles.

# ACKNOWLEDGMENTS

The author wishes to express his appreciation, for their assistance and support, to James Robert Parish and George Butler at Greenwood Press, to the staff and librarians at the University of California, Los Angeles, and the University of Nevada, Las Vegas, and to Josh Stolberg at the University of Southern California. Also, thanks to all the James Dean fans who provided magazine articles and videocassettes.

# JAMES DEAN

# 1

# BIOGRAPHY

Of all the quotable comments uttered or published about James Dean (1931-1955), the most provocative--and prophetic--came not from one of Dean's friends, coworkers, or family members, but from Humphrey Bogart. "He died at just the right time. If he had lived, he'd never have been able to live up to his publicity."

Bogart, whose one meeting with Dean on the set of *East of Eden* (1955) nearly ended in a fight, offered this opinion not long after the tragic news of an auto accident near Cholame, California, was reported on September 30, 1955. James Dean, "promising young newcomer," as he was referred to in more than one obituary, was killed in the accident, his passenger seriously injured, the driver of the other car treated for minor injuries and released. If Bogart's assessment seems unduly pitiless and cynical in the wake of what was unanimously hailed as a tragic episode, its accuracy must also be acknowledged.

James Dean had not yet had the chance to experience much of the dark side of fame. Humphrey Bogart had been a movie star long enough to see how the "Dream Factory" can use and abuse its stars, and how the first failure of a celebrity is greeted with the same glee as the first blush of sucess. Bogart realized that Dean would never have the chance to fail. Having already progressed from actor to icon, he would remain forever handsome, forever sensitive and, most important, forever 24.

But if Dean truly did "die at the right time," he also lived at the right time. In the early 1950s, Hollywood's foremost representation of the American teenager was still Andy Hardy, who was first played on screen by Mickey Rooney in 1937, and whose most serious act of young rebellion was not eating his vegetables. There were more potent examples of alienated youth, but only in exploitation flicks--cheaply made, poorly performed programmers that played for two-weeks at the drive-in. Although John Garfield and Montgomery Clift helped prepare the way, James Dean was the first actor to convey the confusion and adolescent angst experienced to some degree by every teenager. Dean will always be remembered as a fine actor, but as long as teens grapple with first loves, feel misunderstood by their parents, and deal with their first frightening, exciting taste of independence, he will also, always be a symbol of youth in turmoil.

The first Deans came from Kentucky, near the city of Lexington, and settled in Grant County, Indiana around 1815. The Wilsons, including the grandparents of Jimmy Dean's mother, Mildred Marie, arrived at almost the same time. A short, dark-haired farmer's daughter, Mildred, at the age of 19, met dental technician Winton Dean, age 21, and married him on July 26, 1930, not long after discovering that she was pregnant. They moved to Marion, Indiana and took a room at The Seven Gables Apartments.

On Sunday, February 8, 1931, at 2 a.m., Mildred delivered her baby at home, refusing to go to a hospital. Dr. Victor V. Cameron filled out the birth certificate for the eight-pound, ten-ounce boy, and collected a fee of fifteen dollars. His parents chose the name James Byron Dean; James after James Amick, the chief dental officer at the Veterans Administration clinic where Winton worked; Byron was chosen as a tribute to Thomas Byron Vice, Winton's best friend.

It was from Mildred that Jimmy inherited his love for art, poetry, and the stage. They performed skits, sometimes as themselves, sometimes with puppets as actors, for Winton and other members of the family. The happiest moments of Dean's early childhood were spent with his mother, and during visits to the farm in the nearby town of Fairmount, owned by Winton's sister, Ortense, and her husband, Marcus Winslow.

In 1936, Winton was transferred by the V.A. to the Sawtelle Veterans Administration in West Los Angeles, California. Five-year-old Jimmy moved west with his parents, into a five-room apartment in Santa Monica. He attended the McKinley School on Santa Monica Boulevard, and was enrolled by his mother in tapdancing and violin lessons.

Four years later, the family's quiet, comfortable existence was shattered when Mildred was diagnosed with cancer of the uterus. Seven weeks later, on July 14, 1940, Mildred Dean died in the hospital at the age of twenty-nine. Winton and Jimmy were at her bedside. Winton, who had already sold his car to pay for his wife's medical bills, could not afford to attend the funeral in Fairmount.

Jimmy, as any nine-year-old would be, was traumatized by his mother's death. With his grandmother, Emma Dean, he accompanied his mother's body on the train trip from Los Angeles to Fairmount. Every time the train stopped, he would check the baggage car to make sure that the coffin was still there. For the rest of his life, the death of his mother would plunge Dean into bouts of deep depression, anger, and resentment, and prompt a search for surrogate mothers to fill the painful void he felt in his heart.

Winton, still grieving for the loss of his wife, faced a difficult decision regarding his son. "Now, Winton, I want you to think this over carefully," Emma Dean told him. "If you see fit to let Jimmy come back to Fairmount, Ortense and Marcus would like to take him. They'll raise him for you, if you want." Winton, who had to make a living and who did not have a single relative in California, did not want to be separated from his son, but realized that his options were limited; "So far as choosing between the way my sister would mother Jimmy and how some housekeeper might take care of him, there's just no question" (see B110). Eighteen months later, Winton was drafted.

The Winslow farm would seem to many children an idyllic place to grow up. The two-story, fourteen-room white farmhouse was built in 1901, on the edge of a 178-acre lot. There were trees to climb, a porch swing, animals, and a nearby stream that offered fishing in the summer and skating in winter. The small town of Fairmount, population 2,600, had good schools and churches, but no movie theater. The townspeople, most of them Quakers, would not support it.

The house already felt like home to Jimmy, and the Winslows tried their best to ease the boy's transition, including giving him their own bedroom. But Jimmy, who had just lost his mother, now felt abandoned by his father as well. His suffering was waged in silence, and slow to diminish.

Gradually, Jimmy began to find friends in the fourth grade of Fairmount West Ward School, and took to participating in sports and community activities. His excellent grades prompted classmates to nickname him "Quiz Kid." He earned silver and gold medals for speeches he performed for the Women's Christian Temperance Union. He excelled at skating, was a good basketball player despite his diminutive height, and won ribbons for several 4-H projects. He tried to resume violin lessons, but later switched to piano and drums. Charlie Dean, Winton's brother, forged a close relationship with Jimmy, and shared with the boy his love of automobiles.

Charlie bought his first car in 1911, and horrified the town by racing through the streets at 35 miles per hour. According to Emma Dean, Jimmy learned how to drive a tractor first, then a bicycle, and then a bike with a motor called a whizzer. Later, during his sophomore year of high school, he swapped the whizzer for his first motorbike (see B110). Jimmy started hanging out at Marvin Carter's Cycle Shop, and delighted in impressing the others gathered there by racing at 50 miles per hour while lying flat on the saddle.

"If he'd only fallen once, things might have been different," said Marcus Winslow to writer Joe Hyams years later. "Trouble is, he never got hurt, and he never found anything he couldn't do well almost the first time he tried it. Just one fall off the bike and maybe he'd have been afraid of speed, but he was without fear." (see B045)

A natural mimic, Jimmy would entertain Uncle Charlie by aping his movements and mannerisms. His interest in acting never waned since he first performed impromptu shows with his mother. After Mildred Dean, the person who was first to notice Jimmy's talent was Adeline Nall. Nall taught speech and dramatics in junior high and at Fairmount High School. She coached him in dramatic competitions, and admits to "devoting so much class time to her star pupil that difficulties occasionally arose, when other students came to feel that Dean was running the class" (B152).

The teacher-pupil relationship continued through four years of high school. As a freshman, Dean was honored as a playwright as well as an actor in his citizenship class. In 1949, as a senior, Jimmy won the Indiana speech tournament and advanced to the national competition in Longmont, Colorado. Adeline Nall was his coach and chaperon. He placed sixth.

Dean also made the Fairmount High basketball team, and his 40 points over three consecutive games were lauded in the *Fairmount News* sports pages in 1948. He was a letterman in basketball and track, and set a county record in the pole vault that wasn't broken for over 20 years. On May 16, 1949, Dean was asked to read the benediction at commencement, when he graduated with a class of 49 students.

After briefly considering local Earlham College, Dean left for California to live with Winton. His grades weren't high enough for the University of California at Los Angeles (UCLA), so he entered Santa Monica City College for a semester to prepare. Winton, trying perhaps to make up for years of separation, tried to reassert his parental authority by ordering Jimmy to take pre-law courses. Jimmy complied, since Winton was paying his room and board and had bought him a car--a 1939 Chevy sedan--as an early birthday present. However, he also registered for every theater course he could fit into his schedule.

At Santa Monica City College, Dean became an announcer for the school's radio station, and a guard on the college basketball team. Gene Owen, his teacher and counselor, became Dean's first professional acting coach. "He mashed his words together and he was somewhat difficult to understand," recalled Owen (see B255). At first, the blame was placed on his Hoosier accent, but the real culprit was an upper plate Dean wore across his hard palate for a dental problem, which made some tongue positions difficult for certain sounds.

Owen started Jimmy on a semester-long, extra-hour, oral interpretation of *Hamlet*. "I told him that if anything would clear up fuzzy speech it would be the demanding soliloquies of Shakespeare." When he reached the scene in which Hamlet replies to his mother's remark at his seeming dejection over his father's death, Dean, in a dozen lines, "had established a deeply disturbed young Hamlet which touched my heart," Owen recalled. "I had seen the play with every great actor in both England and America in the role, and I had never heard those lines expressed quite so well."

Dean received 'A's in gym and theater, and a 'C' in prelaw. That was enough to convince Winton that Jimmy would never be a lawyer. He consented to his son's desire to enroll in UCLA as a theater arts major. In the summer before his first semester, he appeared in a stock production of *The Romance of Scarlet Gulch* (1949--see S1) under the name Byron James.

He moved out of his father's apartment, and pledged the Epsilon Pi chapter of the Sigma Nu fraternity, mostly because he needed a place to live. It was an uncomfortable situation from the beginning. He was nicknamed "plowboy," for his t-shirt and jeans attire and midwestern accent, and he rarely participated in fraternity events and activities.

Although his first semester at UCLA was not a happy one, Dean auditioned for and won the role of Malcolm in the college's production of *Macbeth*. ". . .the biggest thrill of my life," is how Dean described the experience in a letter to Marcus and Ortense.

In attendance at the last dress rehearsal was a theater arts student named Bill Bast, who would become Dean's best friend for the final six years of Dean's life. His first impression of Dean was not positive--he compared Jimmy's opening-night performance to "an agonizing dental extraction." "His Indiana twang made Shakespeare's immortal lines sound more like they had been written by Mark Twain and were being delivered by Herb Shriner," said Bast years later (see B009). The critic for the UCLA student newspaper also panned Dean; "he failed to show any growth and would have made a hollow king."

Bast was introduced to James Dean by another classmate after *Macbeth* closed. Shortly thereafter, Dean left Sigma Nu, and Bast moved out of the dormitory. They moved into a three-room penthouse in Santa Monica, with a view of the Pacific Ocean. A desperate scramble to raise the $300 rent became a monthly ritual. Bast worked part-time as an usher for CBS television, and Dean had no steady income at all.

Jimmy acquired an agent, Isabelle Draesemer, and was cast in a Pepsi-Cola television commercial for a salary of ten dollars. Dean is one of six happy young adults who laugh and carouse around a jukebox, singing along with the Pepsi jingle. Also appearing in the commercial were Nick Adams and Beverly Long, both of whom would later appear in *Rebel Without a Cause* (1955).

Jerry Fairbanks, the producer of the commercial, arranged an audition with Dean's agent for "Hill Number One," an episode of the TV series *Family Theatre*. Playing John the Apostle, Dean earned $150--his half of the rent--and after this allegorical episode was broadcast at the

Immaculate Heart School, he had acquired his first fan club. Contacting Jimmy through Isabette Draesemer, the Immaculate Heart James Dean Appreciation Society invited Dean to a party in his honor. Jimmy and Bill Bast attended the party, and Dean received his first taste of celebrity adulation.

The week before he began work on "Hill Number One," at an actor's workshop conducted by actor/coach James Whitmore, James Dean showed the first sign of the brilliant actor he would become, according to Bast. The two were given a scene to perform, in which Bast played a jeweler who learns that a watch he received from Dean, playing a customer, had been stolen. Bast's job was to detain Dean until the police arrived; Dean's assignment was to get the watch back and escape. After several tepid run-throughs, Whitmore reminded them of the singleness of purpose that each man should display, and how to achieve that through intense concentration.

"At first, the noticeable change that came over Jimmy was almost frightening," Bast recalled. "With grim determination, he set himself to the desperate task of getting that watch. . .the more demanding and insulting he became, the more emphatic I became in my refusal. The fist fight that resulted had to be broken up by Whitmore and the others." (see B087). "Until then he had understood everything, but now he was able to apply it," Bast recalled. "For the first time, acting made sense to him."

Between acting jobs, Dean worked for awhile with Bast as a CBS usher. He met Beverly Wills, daughter of comedienne Joan Davis, and despite Davis's objections they began dating. The relationship, though short-lived, brought Dean to numerous Hollywood parties, and inspired him to try even harder to prove himself as an actor. He continued to receive roles in television dramas, with the help of new agent Rogers Brackett, and made his film debut in a bit part in Samuel Fuller's Korean War drama, *Fixed Bayonets* (1951) He was on screen for less than a minute in the Dean Martin-Jerry Lewis comedy *Sailor Beware* (1951) and spoke his first line of movie dialogue in the Piper Laurie-Rock Hudson film *Has Anybody Seen My Gal?* (1952).

The restless Dean was not content with the course of his career, and had grown bored with college. He confessed his feelings to James Whitmore, who advised Dean to stop dissipating his energy and talent, and go to New York. "There you will find out whether you can take the uncertainty of an actor's life. . .get to know yourself, and learn how to be yourself" (see B045).

In September of 1951, James Dean arrived in New York City with $150 in his pocket, and a letter of introduction from James Whitmore to director Elia Kazan at The Actors Studio, one of the most prestigious schools in the country. He took a room at a hotel off Times Square, but was so overwhelmed by the size and frenzied pace of New York that, for the first month, he rarely strayed more than three blocks.

Gradually, he developed a small circle of friends, mostly actors who hung out at Cromwell's drugstore in the RCA building, and at Walgreen's in the Paramount building. One of the first was Elizabeth "Dizzy" Sheridan, a struggling dancer who, like Jimmy, was a regular at every open audition in the city.

"He was sitting in the living room (of the Rehersal Club), and I heard him ask a lot of other girls if he could borrow an umbrella, and nobody seemed particularly interested in whether he got wet or not," she recalled of their first meeting. "So I loaned him mine and he was overly grateful" (see B304). Sheridan remembers being unimpressed with Dean at first ("I thought he was a little straggly kid that somebody had brought in"), but their shared interests in art, acting and bullfighting formed the basis of a close friendship.

Within weeks, Jimmy and Dizzy Sheridan were going out every night, to dinner when one of them was working, to the park when money was tight. "He never for one instant thought that he really couldn't make it," said Sheridan. "I mean he always knew that he would one day be a star, and there was no question about it at all."

In February 1953, Dean landed his first acting job since arriving in New York, in an episode of the television series *The Web* entitled "Sleeping Dogs." From 1951 to 1954, he appeared in more than two dozen shows, playing bit parts and later on juvenile leads. Although the persona that would become legendary was formed in these dramas, Dean's television work is often overlooked in assessments of his career, a result perhaps of the infrequent screenings of the material.

Writes Dean fan David Dalton in reviewing this phase of his career, "The mannerisms we associate with the cinematic James Dean are already fully developed: the face flickering with transient emotions, the nervous giggle, hunched shoulders, kabuki eyebrows, dangling cigarette, the fetal curling and feral tensing, the crumpled, imploding body" (see B109).

With the exception of an occasional one-sentence plaudit in a newspaper review, most of these performances, some of which were extraordinary and merit comparison to his work in motion pictures, went largely unheralded by the public. Within the industry, however, James Dean was starting to get noticed.

His first starring role on television was as a small town rebel who becomes a psychopathic killer, in an episode of *Kraft Television Theater* entitled "A Long Time Till Dawn," which aired on November 11, 1953. "Jimmy played the part brilliantly," said Rod Serling, who wrote the teleplay. "I can't imagine anyone playing that particular role better."

Comedian Steve Allen, who hosted a television tribute to James Dean in 1956, recalled the first time he watched Dean work; "His use of authentic hip language, his naturalness, were so impressive that I said to Jayne [Meadows], must find out who directed the show because he's done something absolutely brilliant. No actor I know could speak that language as authentically as this kid. I thought the director must have gotten some boy off the streets and somehow made him play himself" (see B059).

Among Dean's television costars, many of whom were stars or stars-in-the-making, were Anne Jackson (*The Web*, 1952), John Forsythe (*Studio One*, 1953), Cloris Leachman (*Hallmark Hall of Fame*, 1952), John Carradine (*The Kate Smith Show*, 1953), Rod Steiger (*Tales of Tomorrow*, 1953), Jessica Tandy and Hume Cronyn (*Omnibus*, 1953), and Dorothy Gish (*Robert Montgomery Presents*, 1953).

Two of the most significant Dean performances for the small screen, both for *General Electric Theatre*, were aired less than one month apart in late 1953. In "The Dark, Dark Hour," Dean played a gun-toting delinquent who invades the home of a small-town doctor, played by Ronald Reagan. In "I'm a Fool," Dean played a lovestruck farm boy who resorts to deception to impress a beautiful socialite. The girl was played by Dean's future costar in *Rebel Without a Cause*, Natalie Wood.

"I'd heard stories and was frankly afraid of him," Wood recalled years later. Dean entered, a half-hour late, through a large open window, wearing a dirty sport shirt and a pair of jeans with a safety pin attached to the front. "He jumped down on the floor, looked around, picked up a script from the table, and sat in a corner. The director said 'C'mon Jimmy, sit next to Natalie. You're going to have to make love to this girl.' Jimmy didn't even look up. He just grunted" (see B109).

It was performances such as this one, given before the cameras rolled, that formed James Dean's reputation as a difficult, albeit gifted, young actor. Every opportunity to practice his craft brought James Dean the greatest joy he experienced in his brief life, but his behavior on the set left a very different impression. "He had a lousy attitude about working," said Dizzy Sheridan. "He didn't care about rehearsals. He didn't care about the way he dressed. Sometimes he didn't even care about whether he was decent to people or not, as long as he was acting. He felt the *business* of show business was degrading."

Less than two months after Dean met Dizzy Sheridan, Bill Bast moved to New York City and met Jimmy for coffee at Walgreen's. Once again they became roommates, in a single room with bath at the Iroquois Hotel on 44th Street. Before that, Dean had been living with Rogers Brackett, who was living next door at the Algonquin. Brackett, as he had in Los Angeles, opened doors of casting offices for Dean, and was primarily responsible for Jimmy's first "big break," his casting in the Broadway play *See the Jaguar* (1952--see S6).

The relationship between Dean and Brackett, fifteen years his senior, has been characterized as a "West Hollywood rendering of Professor Henry Higgins and Eliza Doolittle" (see B109). "My primary interest in Jimmy was as an actor. His talent was so obvious. Secondarily, I loved him, and Jimmy loved me. If it was a father-son relationship, it was also somewhat incestuous," Brackett told Ronald Martinetti in the book *The James Dean Story* (see B051).

James Dean's bisexuality is now accepted by most authors and film historians, but what is still debated is whether Dean pursued his relationships with men for pleasure, or to further his career. The one-night stands at Hollywood parties alleged in various Dean biographies are most often characterized as "casting couch" hurdles. Not one man appears on any biographer's list of Dean's genuine paramours; his "one true love," if indeed he had one, was MGM starlet Pier Angeli. When film stardom loomed for Dean in 1955, he cut all ties with Rogers Brackett, despite the risk of subsequent exposure.

Through Brackett, Dean met producer Lemuel Ayers and his wife, Shirley. Aware that the Ayers' were developing *See the Jaguar* for Broadway, Dean spent several weekends at their home and on their yacht, never once revealing that he was an actor. It was a calculated move that worked--after Dean casually mentioned his classes at The Actors Studio at the conclusion of a week-long cruise to Cape Cod, Lemuel Ayers invited him to read for the play.

Brackett also introduced Dean to Jane Deacy, who became the actor's next agent. It was Deacy who, in September of 1955, negotiated James Dean's movie contract with Warner Bros. He called her "Mom," as did some of her other clients, but with Jimmy the term was used more sincerely. His longing for an affectionate parental role model had not abated since he accompanied his mother's casket on the train from Los Angeles to Fairmount, Indiana.

Leonard Rosenman, who composed the music for *East of Eden* and *Rebel Without a Cause*, was another of Dean's friends in New York and, despite being just seven years older than Dean, also became a surrogate parent. "He asked me to come out and play ball with him," Rosenman recalled. "I said no. . .he kept insisting and finally I shouted in exasperation: 'You know I don't like sports. Why the hell is it so important that I play ball with you?' Stammering, he replied, 'It's. . .like. . .you want your father to play ball with you'" (see B282).

For his audition to The Actors Studio, Dean performed an original scene entitled "Ripping Off Layers to Find Roots," written by another aspiring student, Christine White, whom he met in Jane Deacy's office. Out of 150 applicants, Dean and White were two of the fifteen applicants who were accepted as members. Dean, at the age of 21, was the youngest student in the history of the Studio.

His stay, however, was short-lived. He appeared in in-house

productions of *End as a Man*, *The Sea Gull* and *Aria da Capo*, but after teacher Lee Strasberg lambasted his performance of a scene from a play called *Matador*, his attitude changed. After not attending classes at all for several days, Dean returned to The Actors Studio, but was no longer eager to participate in scenes and exercises.

"It was my feeling that he didn't go far enough," Strasberg said later of his critique. "It seemed. . .that he was not using enough of himself" (see B030). However, Dean's brief tenure at the Studio was pivotal to his future, for it was here that he first met Elia Kazan, who would later direct *East of Eden*.

Before he was offered the chance to read for *See the Jaguar*, Dean was unemployed for much of the summer of 1952, as were Bill Bast and Dizzy Sheridan. A desire for home cooked meals prompted a trip to Fairmount to visit Jimmy's family. The trio hitchhiked from New York to Indiana.

They spent two weeks at the Winslow farm, where Bill Bast saw a side to his friend he had not yet encountered. "It was a wonderful thing to watch him touch once again the gentle roots of his early years," Bast recalled (see B009). He spent hours talking with his cousin, Markie, and introduced Bill and Dizzy to Adeline Nall.

Back in New York, Dean read for and won a role in Lemuel Ayers' *See the Jaguar*.  Rehearsal began on October 20, 1952, and the play opened on Broadway at the Cort Theatre on December 3. Reviews of out-of-town tryouts had been mostly negative, though Jimmy was cited as a promising newcomer.

Dean played sixteen-year-old Wally Wilkins, a rural lad who spent most of his youth imprisoned in an icehouse by his unbalanced mother. Released to the outside world after his mother's death, Wally is stalked by a deranged pet shop owner. New York critics panned the script ("accomplishes nothing but noise and confusion," observed the *New York Times*), but praised the performances of Dean and costar Arthur Kennedy. Although the play closed after just five performances, the exposure Dean received led to numerous offers of television work, and the opportunity to fly to Hollywood for a screen test. Dean turned it down, hoping for more stagework in New York.

The year of 1953 was Jimmy's busiest as an actor. He appeared in sixteen television dramas, and on stage in *The Scarecrow* at New York's off-Broadway Theatre de Lys. The play, which starred Patricia Neal, Eli Wallach and Anne Jackson, was a revival of a 1908 drama about a scarecrow brought to life by the devil. It closed after six performances.

In December, 1953, Jane Deacy sent Jimmy to audition for *The Immoralist*, a play based on Andre Gide's novel, and adapted by Ruth and Augustus Goetz. Louis Jourdan and Geraldine Page starred as newlyweds Michel and Marcelline, whose honeymoon in Africa is

witnesses to this display, the story has yet to be confirmed or denied with any certainty.

Pier Angeli gave birth to a boy, Perry Rocco Luigi Damone, eight months after her marriage, and two months before the death of James Dean. The fact that Pier had still been seeing Jimmy as late as two weeks before her wedding has fueled some intriguing speculation. In August of 1957 she separated from Damone, and the couple divorced one year later. A long, bitter custody battle ensued--both parents were accused of kidnapping at different times, before Pier received sole custody in 1965. In September, 1971, she died from an overdose of barbiturates.

Stunned by the end of his relationship with Pier, Jimmy was even more unprepared to face the oncoming spotlight of national celebrity. Even before the release of *East of Eden*, Hollywood columnists had begun touting James Dean as the heir to Marlon Brando, a brooding heartthrob with a raw, prodigious talent. Dean, still contemptuous of showbiz hype, did nothing to encourage this attention. "I came to Hollywood to act, not to charm society," he told *Hollywood Citizen-News* columnist Sidney Skolsky. Two days before *Eden*'s world premiere at the New York Paramount Theatre, on March 9, 1955, Dean had already slipped quietly back to Los Angeles.

Rather than make the rounds of star-studded parties with studio-arranged escorts, Dean spent many of his evenings at Googie's, a coffee shop on Sunset Boulevard. There, he chatted with a small circle of friends that included Maila Nurmi, best-known for her horror movie hostess alter-ego, Vampira, singer Eartha Kitt, and actors Dennis Hopper and Nick Adams, both of whom appeared in *Rebel Without a Cause*.

His "movie-star abode," according to friend John Gilmore, was a furnished single apartment above Sunset; "one room with a kitchen, littered with paper cups and takeout orders from drive-ins and Googie's. Stacks of papers, spools of recording tape, and his clothes were thrown in the closet" (see B130).

Having kept his promise to Elia Kazan about riding his motorcycle, Dean celebrated the final day of shooting on *East of Eden* by trading in his Triumph T-110 cycle for the more powerful Triumph 500. After the film was released, he purchased a white Porsche 356, 1,500 cc Super Speedster convertible. Two months later, he was already shopping for a faster model.

Warner Bros. renewed Jimmy's six-month contract, and on January 4, 1955, the studio announced that Dean had been cast in *Rebel Without a Cause*. After just one starring role, he had progressed from unknown actor, happy for a job, to a hot commodity who could afford to be selective. *Rebel* director Nicholas Ray had to convince Jimmy that the film would have more resonance than its drive-in genre story would suggest, and that it was a worthy follow-up to an adaptation of John

Steinbeck.

Ray and the cast assembled at the Chateau Marmont Hotel for script readings, where Dean became reacquainted with Natalie Wood. Though they would convincingly play young lovers in *Rebel*, seventeen-year-old Natalie was having an affair with her 44-year-old director.

Before production officially began on March 28, James Dean made his last trip back home to Fairmount, Indiana. Accompanied by photographer Dennis Stock, Dean attended the Fairmount High Sweethearts Ball on Valentine's Day, and posed for a series of pictures that accompanied an article in *Life* Magazine. "Moody New Star" was the headline of the Dean story that appeared in the March 7, 1955 issue, just two days prior to the premiere of *East of Eden*.

Dean returned to Hollywood on March 6. On April 14, Warner Bros. announced that he had been signed to play boxer Rocky Graziano in the MGM film *Somebody Up There Likes Me*. MGM obtained Dean's services by exercising a contract option that stemmed from the studio's loaning of Elizabeth Taylor to Warner Bros. for *Giant* (1956). Of more pressing interest to Dean was his upcoming road race in Santa Barbara. He had competed for the first time on March 26 at the Palm Springs Road Races, won his preliminary race, and finished second in the main event. "In those days, racing was what he cared about the most," his friend Bill Hickman told the *Los Angeles Times* in 1973. "If he had lived, he might have become a champion driver."

On May 1, Dean competed at Minter Field in Bakersfield, and placed third in 750-1,500 cc modified race. At the Santa Barbara Road Races, Jimmy started eighteenth, and had charged all the way to fourth place when his Porsche blew a piston. The car's failure, combined with his coming up short of the checkered flag in previous races, prompted Dean to go car shopping once more. There was another race in Salinas on October 2, and he was going to be ready.

*Rebel Without a Cause* wrapped up production on May 26, and five days later Dean joined the cast of his next film, *Giant*, in Marfa, Texas. The contrast between the two filmmaking experiences would prove to be profound; in *Rebel*, Dean played Jim Stark, a contemporary teenager yearning for the love and acceptance of his family and peers. In *Giant*, the film adaptation of Edna Ferber's novel, he was to play Jett Rink, a jealous, embittered ranchhand who strikes it rich. The role would require him to age 40 years.

The filming of *Rebel* was a collaborative effort; Dean's improvisations were not only tolerated but encouraged by director Nicholas Ray, whom Dean looked upon as a kindred spirit. The cast included several of Jimmy's closest friends, including Natalie Wood, Dennis Hopper, Corey Allen, Steffi Sidney, and Nick Adams.

*Giant* was moviemaking the old-fashioned way, with megastars

Elizabeth Taylor and Rock Hudson in the leads, and veteran director George Stevens at the helm. "He hated (Stevens), didn't think he was a good director, and he was always angry and full of contempt," said Hudson of Dean years later (see B174). While "hate" might be too severe of a description, it is true that Dean ignored his call times and, on July 23, chose not to show up for work at all.

Elizabeth Taylor was Dean's closest friend on the set; the two had already met when Taylor visited the set of *Rebel Without a Cause*, and Dean gave her a ride around the Warners backlot in his Porsche. "We had an extraordinary friendship," said Taylor on *Good Morning America*. "We would sometimes sit up until three in the morning, and he would tell me about his past, his mother, minister, his loves, and the next day he would just look straight through me as if he'd given or revealed too much of himself."

A few weeks before production ended on *Giant*, Taylor bought Jimmy a Siamese kitten, whom he named Marcus. His affection for the kitten was observed by everyone on the set, so it came as a surprise to the cast and crew when he gave Marcus away. "When they asked him why, he replied that he was too concerned for his friend and realized that he led such a strange and unpredictable life that some night he might just never come home again. 'Then,' he asked, 'what would happen to Marcus?'"

On September 17, 1955, Dean taped a public service announcement for the National Safety Council. In it, actor Gig Young asks Jimmy about his racing career, and for his opinion about fast driving on the highway. "I took a lot of unnecessary chances on the highway," Dean replies. "Then I started racing and, uh, now when I drive on the highways I'm extra cautious. No one knows what they're doing half the time. . .I don't have the urge to speed on the highway. People think racing is dangerous. But I'll take my chances on the track any day than on a highway."

"Wait a minute, Jimmy," Young says as Dean turns to leave. "Do you have any special advice for the young people who drive?" "Take it easy," says Dean. "The life you might save might be mine!"

Four days after taping the commercial, Dean purchased a Porsche 550 Spyder from Competition Motors in Hollywood. The car was one of 75 that had been imported by owner Johnny von Neumann directly from the factory in Germany; the tiny, aluminum-bodied racer, with a ladder frame and a midship-mounted, four-cam, air-cooled four, was built for privateer racers.

According to *Car and Driver*, the 550 Spyder was the best small-displacement racer in the world. "Not only was it quick and nimble, but its anvil-like reliability helped win many high placings in major endurance races. There was some question whether Dean was experienced enough for the machine, but on September 21 von Neumann accepted his check for $3000, plus Dean's 356 Speedster in trade, for Spyder number 550-0055" (see B334). Dean then brought the car to George Barris, who customized the Spyder with red stripes, Dean's racing number, 130, on the doors, hood and rear deck, and the words "Little Bastard" in script across the tail.

Like Elia Kazan before him, George Stevens had banned Dean from high-speed driving while *Giant* was in production. Now that his work was finished, except for some dialogue looping he could deal with later, Dean was free to enter the race in Salinas. The small produce town was best known as the birthplace of John Steinbeck, which Dean must have considered a good omen.

Rolf Wutherich, a German mechanic who worked for von Neumann, prepared the Spyder for competition. Because of Jimmy's inexperience at the controls, Wutherich suggested that they make the 300-mile journey to Salinas together, while someone else ferried Dean's 1953 Ford station wagon and a borrowed trailer for the return trip.

On the morning of September 30, 1955, James Dean left the home he was leasing in Sherman Oaks, and arrived at Competition Motors a little after eight. He talked racing with the salesmen and mechanics, then left to have lunch at the Farmer's Market with his father and his Uncle Charlie, who had introduced Jimmy to the joys of racing. After lunch, he returned to Competition Motors to pick up Wutherich.

They set out on Sepulveda Boulevard to Route 99 (now known as Interstate 5). The plan was to head north on Route 99 into the San Joaquin Valley, then west on Route 166 toward Taft and Maricopa; then north on 33 to Blackwell's Corner. From there it was a straight drive west on 466 into Paso Robles. At about 3:30 p.m., Jimmy was stopped by a California Highway Patrolman for driving 65 m.p.h. in a 55 m.p.h. zone.

At 5:45 p.m., Dean was cruising the long straightaway approaching Routes 46 and 41 in Cholame. Heading east was a 23-year-old California Polytechnic student named Donald Turnupseed, who was on his way home to Fresno for the weekend. He turned his 1950 Ford left off 466 where Route 41 angled northeast--directly in front of the Spyder. According to Wutherich, Dean's last words were "He's gotta see us. He's gotta stop."

Dean realized it was too late to use the brakes, and tried instead to accelerate around the Ford, but to no avail. The Spyder took the full impact of the Ford's grille in the driver's side door. Wutherich was thrown clear of the wreck. Turnupseed was dazed and bloodied, but essentially unhurt. Dean was crammed against the steering wheel and mauled by the front of Turnupseed's car. His neck was broken, his body shattered.

An ambulance, the only one in Cholame, arrived promptly after eyewitnesses called for help. Dean's body was released from the wreckage and raced to the emergency room of the Paso Robles War Memorial Hospital, where he was pronounced dead on arrival. Turnupseed told police that he did not see the Porsche, and was not charged in the accident. Despite attempts at revisionist history in books such as The Death of James Dean (seeB010), the tragedy of James Dean's death can only be blamed on James Dean.

Dean's body was taken from the hospital to the Kuehl Funeral Home in Paso Robles; the Spyder, along with Turnupseed's Ford, were towed to a Quonset-hut garage in Cholame. Less than one hour after the accident, local radio station KPRL was reporting the news of James Dean's death. Donald Turnupseed wound up hitchhiking back to the town of Tulare. In the 40 years that have passed since the accident, he never granted an interview or written his account of that fateful night. Turnupseed died of lung cancer in July of 1995.

The phone rang at Warner Bros. a few minutes after 6 p.m.. A studio policeman took the call from the Paso Robles Hospital, and contacted the publicity department. Giant producer Henry Ginsberg was among the first to learn of the tragedy. He called George Stevens, who was then screening the day's rushes for Elizabeth Taylor, Rock Hudson, and Carroll Baker. Stevens relayed the news; "Ladies and gentlemen, I have an announcement to make. There's been a crash. Jimmy Dean has been killed."

On October 4, the body of James Dean was returned to Fairmount, Indiana. On October 8, the funeral was held at the Back Creek Friends Church. More than 3,000 people attended the services, but thousands more around the world mourned his passing. On October 26, Rebel Without a Cause premiered in New York, earning rave reviews for Dean's performance and confirming his coronation as an icon of misunderstood youth. "As a farewell performance, (Dean) leaves behind, with this film, genuine artistic regret," wrote Variety, "for here was a talent which might have touched the heights."

At the time of his death, the James Dean estate consisted of two pairs of cuff links, one traveling clock, a wristwatch, a perfume flask, an I.D. bracelet, three racing trophies, one rifle, one set of three bongo drums, one red leather suitcase, and a pair of bull's horns and a matador's cape. Dean did not live long enough to draft a will, but one week before his death he took out a $100,000 life insurance policy. His intentions for the policy were not finalized, so the entire sum was awarded to his father.

The stories that filled newspapers and magazines in the months that followed the accident expressed sorrow, shock, and a fascination with the ghoulish devotion of his legion of fans. "Up to 8,000 letters a month are addressed to Dean, more than go to any other Hollywood name these days," Life magazine reported in September of 1956. "Most of the letters are from teenagers. . .a good many letter writers want something that belonged to Dean, from a lock of his hair to a piece of his smashed car."

Tribute songs were recorded. Dozens of one-shot magazines satisfied the public's hunger for any new information about the life and death of James Dean. Fan clubs were formed. Merchandisers trafficked in red windbreaker jackets and other Dean-related items, all without legal approval.

George Stevens received letters warning him not to cut out as much as one single frame of Dean from *Giant*. "It's absolutely weird," Stevens said, "the most uncomfortable stuff I've ever read." The tabloids chimed in with their own bizarre takes on the tragedy. Vampira was accused of causing his death through black magic; "Ghost drivers" racing through the night along the road to Cholame; the curse of James Dean's "death car."

To be fair, however, the Spyder did have a rather colorful history following the crash and, whether by coincidence or curse, more than one person who came in contact with the car died prematurely. After the Porsche's remains were taken to San Luis Obispo, racing enthusiast Dr. William Eschrich of Burbank bought the undamaged engine and transaxle, which he installed in his Lotus 9. "I have no special feeling about it," he told *Newsweek*. " I just wish the motor could go faster." One year later, Eschrich was involved in a car crash that killed his friend, Dr. Troy McHenry, who had also been driving a car equipped with parts from Dean's Porsche. Rolf Wutherich was killed in a traffic accident in 1981, at the age of 53.

George Barris obtained the rest of the wreck, and donated it to the Greater Los Angeles Safety Council. The car was sent on a four-year nationwide tour, during which patrons could pay 50 cents to sit behind the wheel. In 1960, the Spyder was stolen during a train trip from Florida to California, and has yet to be found. A brisk black market in alleged pieces from the Porsche still flourishes.

James Dean's name was prominent in the press throughout 1956. On February 18, he received a posthumous Academy Award nomination for his performance in *East of Eden*. At the ceremony on March 21, he lost to Ernest Borgnine in *Marty*. *Giant* premiered in New York on October 10. Since Dean never made it back to Warners to loop his dialogue for the Jett Rink banquet scene, his voice was dubbed by actor Nick Adams. For his performance Dean earned a second Academy Award nomination, but lost to Yul Brynner in *The King and I*.

Overnight, Fairmount, Indiana, was transformed from a sleepy midwestern town to a popular vacation destination. Fans make the "pilgrimage" to Dean's hometown on his birthday and the anniversary of his death, to visit his grave (the headstone of which has been stolen more than once), the Winslow farm, and his drama teacher, Adeline Nall.

"There were only two people in the '50s. There was Elvis Presley, who changed the music, and James Dean, who really changed our lives," said actor Martin Sheen, in Fairmount on September 30, 1980. Thousands of fans turned out for a 25th anniversary tribute, which included the unveiling of a plaque in the Fairmount High School auditorium. The James Dean Gallery, a collection of photographs and memorabilia, was opened in Fairmount in 1988. Monuments to the actor have been erected at Griffith Park, where part of *Rebel Without a Cause* was filmed, at Cholame near the sight of the accident, and as far away as Paris, France. Warner Bros. still receives an average of 500 Dean-related letters every week.

By 1991, more than 250 companies had registered items from the James Dean Foundation, formed by Dean's family and the Curtis Management Group. Jackets, Stetson hats, sunglasses, t-shirts, posters, jigsaw puzzles, calendars, figurines, and Hallmark greeting cards emblazoned with Dean's image sell in numbers comparable to those remembering Elvis and Marilyn Monroe. In 1990, the Foundation earned almost $6 million. "Not bad," observed author Joe Hyams, "considering Dean's salary for *Rebel Without a Cause* was $10,000."

In 1993, Curtis Management Group won a lawsuit it had filed against Warner Bros. The studio had claimed that its standard artist contract with Dean gave it merchandising rights to the actor's name and likeness. A judge did not agree, and awarded Curtis $1.6 million.

Four decades after his death, James Dean is having "one of the busiest years of his career," reported *Scarlet Street* magazine in its Winter, 1995 issue. A new biography, the 25th, enjoyed brisk sales, and production began on two film biographies.

James Dean in 1954. (Photograph courtesy of Photofest)

# 2

# CHRONOLOGY

1931    **February 8**--James Byron Dean is born in the Marion, Indiana, home of his parents, Winton and Mildred Dean, at 2 a.m.

1933    **July 5**--The Dean family moves from Marion, Indiana to the nearby community of Fairmount, Indiana.

1935    **June 7**--The family moves to Santa Monica, California, after Winton Dean is transferred to the Sawtelle Veterans' Hospital.

1940    **July 14**--Mildred Dean dies of cancer in Los Angeles.

        **July 20**--James Dean returns to Fairmount, on the same train that carries his mother's body. He moves in with his aunt and uncle, Ortense and Marcus Winslow.

1947    **March 28**--Fairmount High School sophomore James Dean plays the title character in the play *Mooncalf Mugford*, his first public acting performance. More school plays follow.

1949    **April 9**--Dean wins first prize in the National Forensic League's state contest, held in Peru, Indiana, for his recitation of "A Madman's Manuscript," from Charles Dickens' *The Pickwick Papers*. He placed sixth on the national level.

        **May 19**--Forty-nine students, among them James Dean, graduate from Fairmount High School.

        **June 15**--Dean buys a one-way bus ticket to Los Angeles, California.

        **September 6**--enters Santa Monica City College.

1950    **September 5**--enters the University of California, Los Angeles.

**November 29**--Dean plays Malcolm in a UCLA Theatre production of *Macbeth*.

**December 13**--first professional acting job; Dean appears in a television commercial for Pepsi-Cola, filmed in Los Angeles' Griffith Park.

1951    **January**--drops out of UCLA.

**March 25**--Dean makes his dramatic television debut in *Hill Number One*.

**July 22**--plays bit part in the film *Fixed Bayonets*.

**August**--plays bit parts in two films, *Has Anybody Seen My Gal* and *Sailor Beware*.

**October**--moves to New York City.

1952    **February 20**--appears in "Sleeping Dogs" episode of the television series *The Web*.

**March 3**--appears in episode of *Studio One*, entitled "Ten Thousand Horses Singing."

**March 17**--appears in a *Lux Video Theatre* episode entitled "The Foggy, Foggy Dew."

**May 21**--appears in "Prologue to Glory" episode of *Kraft Television Theatre*.

**May 26**--appears on *Studio One* in episode entitled "Abraham Lincoln."

**June 2**--appears in *Hallmark Hall of Fame* production of "Forgotten Children."

**August**--Dean auditions for acting coach Lee Strasberg, and is accepted into The Actors Studio.

**December 3**--makes his Broadway debut in *See the Jaguar* (three performances).

1953   **January 15**--appears in the dramatic presentation "Hound of Heaven," on television's *The Kate Smith Show*.

**January 29**--appears on television series *Treasury Men in Action*.

**February 8**--appears on *You Are There*, in an episode entitled "The Capture of Jesse James."

**April 14**--first of four appearances on television series *Danger*.

**April 16**--appears on *Treasury Men in Action*.

**May 1**--appears on *Tales of Tomorrow* episode entitled "The Evil Within."

**July 17**--appears in *Campbell Soundstage* episode entitled "Something For an Empty Briefcase."

**August 17**--appears in "Sentence of Death," on *Studio One Summer Theatre*.

**August 25**--second appearance on *Danger*.

**September 11**--appears on television series *The Big Story*.

**October 4**--appears in William Inge's teleplay "Glory in Flower" on *Omnibus*.

**October 14**--On *Kraft Television Theatre*, Dean appears in the episode "Keep Our Honor Bright."

**October 16**--appears on episode of *Campbell Soundstage* entitled "Life Sentence."

**November 11**--appears in Rod Serling teleplay "A Long Time Till Dawn," on the series *Kraft Television Theatre*.

**November 17**--appears on *Armstrong Circle Theatre*, in an episode entitled "The Bells of Cockaigne."

**November 23**--appears in "Harvest," an episode of *Robert Montgomery Presents*.

1954    **February**--appears in off-Broadway dramatic reading of *Woman of Trachis*.

       **February 8**--*The Immoralist*, costarring James Dean, begins its 104-performance run on Broadway.

       **February 16**--Dean films a screen test for *East of Eden*.

       **February 23**--gives his last performance in *The Immoralist*.

       **March 5**--Warner Bros. announces the casting of James Dean in *East of Eden*.

       **March 30**--makes his third appearance on *Danger*.

       **April 7**--signs contract with Warner Bros.

       **June**--meets Pier Angeli on the Warner Bros. lot.

       **July 6**--Dean acquires a California driver's license.

       **September 5**--Now back in New York, Dean appears in an episode of *Philco TV Playhouse* entitled "Run Like a Thief."

       **November 9**--makes his fourth appearance on *Danger*.

       **November 14**--appears opposite Natalie Wood in *General Electric Theatre* episode entitled "I'm A Fool."

       **November 24**--Pier Angeli marries singer Vic Damone.

       **December 12**--appears opposite Ronald Reagan in *General Electric Theatre* episode entitled "The Dark, Dark Hour."

1955    **January 4**--On the same day that Warner Bros. announces the casting of James Dean in *Rebel Without a Cause*, Dean appears as a troubled youth in "The Thief," an episode of *The U.S. Steel Hour*.

       **March 10**--*East of Eden* opens.

       **March 28**--*Rebel Without a Cause* begins shooting.

       **May 6**--appears in *Schlitz Playhouse of Stars* episode entitled

"The Unlighted Road."

**May 26**--last day of *Rebel* shooting.

**June 3**--Dean joins cast of *Giant*, already shooting in Marfa, Texas.

**September 17**--films public service television commercial  for the National Safety Council, warning against fast driving.

**September 21**--Dean buys a silver Porsche 550 Spyder.

**September 30**--at approximately 5:45 p.m., James Dean is killed when his Porsche collides with a Ford sedan driven by Donald Turnupseed.

**October 8**--funeral at Fairmount, Indiana.

**October 26**--*Rebel Without a Cause* opens.

1956    Publication of William Bast's biography *James Dean*.

**February 18**--Dean is nominated for an Academy Award as Best Actor (*East of Eden*).

**October 10**--*Giant* opens.

**October 14**--tributes to James Dean are broadcast both on *The Ed Sullivan Show* and *The Steve Allen Show*.

1957    **February 18**--Dean is nominated for an Academy Award as Best Actor (*Giant*).

1974    Publication of *The Films of James Dean* by Mark Whitman, *James Dean: A Short Life* by Venable Herndon, and *James Dean: The Mutant King* by David Dalton.

1975    Publication of *James Dean: A Biography* by John Howlett, *The James Dean Story* by Ronald Martinetti, and *The Real James Dean* by John Gilmore.

1978    Publication of *James Dean Revisited* by Dennis Stock.

1982    Publication of *James Dean: A Portrait* by Roy Schatt.

1983    Publication of *James Dean* by Beulah and Sanford Roth, *James Dean is Not Dead* by Stephen Morrissey, and *James Dean: The Way it Was* by Terry Cunningham.

1984    Publication of *The Last James Dean Book* by Dante Volpe, *Rebels United* by Joel Brean, and *James Dean: American Icon* by David Dalton and Ron Cayen.

1985    **September 30**--James Dean Day in Los Angeles.

1986    Publication of *James Dean: Footsteps of a Giant* by Wolfgang Fuchs and *The Death of James Dean* by Warren Newton Beath.

1987    Publication of *James Dean on Location* by Marceau Devillers.

1988    **November 1**--unveiling of James Dean monument in Griffith Park.

1989    Publication of *Wish You Were Here, Jimmy Dean* by Martin Dawber and *James Dean: In His Own Words* by Mick St. Michael.

1990    Publication of *James Dean: Shooting Star* by Barney Hoskyns and David Loehr and *James Dean: Behind the Scene* by Leith Adams and Keith Burns.

1991    Publication of *The Unabridged James Dean* by Randall Riese.

1992    Publication of *James Dean: Little Boy Lost* by Joe Hyams.

1994    Publication of *Boulevard of Broken Dreams* by Paul Alexander.

# 3

# STAGE WORK

**S 1  THE ROMANCE OF SCARLET GULCH** (The Miller Playhouse Theatre Guild, Los Angeles, 1949.)

**Commentary**
Sometime between June 15 and September 6, 1949, Eighteen-year-old James Dean played a small role in a summer stock musical production of *The Romance of Scarlet Gulch*. He was billed under the name Byron James.

**S 2  SHE WAS ONLY A FARMER'S DAUGHTER** (Santa Monica City College, Santa Monica, California, May 1, 1950. 1 performance.)

**Commentary**
James Dean spent two semesters--fall, 1949 and spring, 1950--at Santa Monica City College, where he hoped to improve his grades enough to gain admission to the University of California, Los Angeles (UCLA). He joined the drama club, and appeared in a department production of *She Was Only a Farmer's Daughter*, presented as part of the school's 1950 May Day festivities. Dick Mangan, Nancy McGrath, Rosemary Cicco, Allan Light, Betty Youst, Ellen Sidman and Ann McCormack were among the other student cast members.

**S 3  MACBETH** (Royce Hall, University of California, Los Angeles, Los Angeles, California , November 29,1950. 4 performances.)

**Reviews**
"Malcolm (played by sophomore James Dean) failed to show any growth,

and would have made a hollow king." (*Spotlight*, UCLA, December 1950)

## Commentary
James Dean transferred from Santa Monica City College to UCLA in September, 1950. He auditioned for and won the role of Malcolm in the school's production of Shakespeare's tragedy, *Macbeth*, and described the experience in a letter to his aunt and uncle as "the biggest thrill of my life." (see B045). The school's newspaper was not kind to Dean in its review. Bill Bast, Dean's friend and fellow theatre arts student, compared the opening night performance to "an agonizing dental extraction." "He performed the role with the most dreadful Indiana accent, a terrible farm-boy twang," recalled Bast. "He couldn't pronounce the Shakespeare, couldn't get his tongue around it." In February of 1951, after being turned down for a role in a production of *The Dark of the Moon*, Dean left UCLA to pursue an acting career full-time.

## S 4   THE ACTORS STUDIO (In-house productions, New York City, 1952-1953.)

## Commentary
In the summer of 1952, 21-year-old James Dean became the youngest member in the history of the Actors Studio. His attendance in class was sporadic and he left in less than a year, but during his time at the school Dean appeared in three in-house productions.

In Edna St. Vincent Millay's *Aria da Capo*, Dean played the role of Pierrot in a production directed by Fred Stewart. In Anton Chekhov's *The Sea Gull*, he played outcast writer Konstantin Treplev, opposite Joseph Anthony as Trigorin. *End as a Man*, by Calder Willingham, ranks with the Studio's most successful productions. Directed by Jack Garfein and starring Ben Gazzarra, Albert Salmi, Pat Hingle, Arthur Storch, Paul Richards, William Smithers, and James Dean in the role of Starkson, the play was presented three times during May and June, 1953, and was successful enough to move off-Broadway. However, when *End as a Man* opened at the Theatre de Lys in Greenwich Village on September 15, 1953, Dean was working steadily in television and had dropped out of the cast.

## S 5   THE METAMORPHOSIS (The Village Theatre, New York City, August 1952. 1 performance.)

## Commentary
James Dean was among the actors, some of whom were fellow students at the Actors Studio, who participated in a dramatic reading of Franz

Kafka's *The Metamorphosis*. The off-Broadway reading was not reviewed, and is omitted from most Dean biographies.

**S 6    SEE THE JAGUAR** (Previews at the Parsons Theatre in New Haven, Connecticut, in November, 1952. Opened in New York City at The Cort Theatre on December 3, 1952. 5 performances.)

**Credits**
Directed by Michael Gordon; Written by N. Richard Nash; Produced by Lemuel Ayers, in association with Helen Jacobson; Music by Alec Wilder; Scenery and costumes by Lemuel Ayers

**Cast**
Phillip Pine (Hilltop), David Clarke (Yetter), Constance Ford (Janna), Roy Fant (Gramfa Ricks), Margaret Barker (Mrs. Wilkins), Arthur Kennedy (Dave Ricks), Cameron Prud'homme (Brad), George Tyne (Harvey), Arthur Batanides (Frank), Ted Jacques (Meeker), Florence Sundstrom (Mrs. Meeker), JAMES DEAN (Wally Wilkins), Dane Knell (Jee Jee), Harrison Dowd (Sam), Harry Bergman (Andy), Tony Kraber (Carson)

**Synopsis**
In a small town in the rural south, sixteen-year-old Wally Wilkins is kept in an icehouse by his unbalanced mother, who wants to protect him from life's harsh realities. Before she dies, Wally's mother releases her son, barefoot and completely naive about the outside world. Brad, the cruel town landlord, owns a bizarre pet store in which he displays the wild animals he has captured. Hanging over every cage is a smug tribute to his success--"See the Ocelot," "See the Weasel." His next objective is to capture a jaguar, for which a cage has already been prepared. But after discovering that Wally may be in line for a substantial inheritance, Brad sets out to capture Wally as well.

Wally is sheltered from Brad's clutches by a young couple, Dave and Janna Ricks, who were acquainted with his mother. As the chase progresses, Wally is attacked by the jaguar and kills it in self-defense. Brad, outraged at the loss of his prey, locks Wally in the cage that was intended for the jaguar.

**Reviews**
"If *See the Jaguar* had a reasonably credible story, it would be the best new piece on Broadway--but it hasn't, so it isn't. As the boy, James Dean is very good." (*New York Daily News*, December 4, 1952)

"James Dean adds an extraordinary performance in an almost impossible role: that of a bewildered lad who has been completely shut off from a vicious world by an overzealous mother and who is coming upon both the beauty and the brutality of the mountain for the first time. It is the author's bad luck--and ours, too--that so much that is striking finally goes down the drain of an over-insistent symbolism." (*New York Herald-Tribune*, December 4, 1952)

"*See the Jaguar* accomplishes nothing but noise and confusion. Taking their cue from (N. Richard Nash's) tortured literary style and tangled craftsmanship, the cast all work their heads off. . . but nothing understandable comes out of the performance." (*New York Times*, December 4, 1952)

## Additional Reviews
*New York Daily Mirror* (December 4, 1952); *New York Journal American* (December 4, 1952); *New York Post* (December 4, 1952); *New York World-Telegram and Sun* (December 4, 1952)

## Commentary
In the summer of 1952, James Dean accompanied his agent, Rogers Brackett, to a cocktail party hosted by producer Lemuel Ayers. Brackett had already been told that Ayers had a new play in production, and set about charming the producer, without ever mentioning that he was an aspiring actor. Dean became friends with Ayers and his wife, Shirley, and while accompanying them on a week-long cruise to Cape Cod he casually mentioned his intention to study at the Actors Studio. As Dean had hoped, he was invited to audition for Ayers' play, *See the Jaguar.*

Over one hundred other actors read for the role of Wally Wilkins, but it was James Dean who most impressed Ayers and the play's author, N. Richard Nash. "He was the only person in the play who caught the spirit of it from the beginning," said Nash. "He brought a great richness to the part. There are scenes of great puzzlement, and you have never seen such puzzlement as portrayed by Dean. He had it. It was deep down and quite beautiful." (see B044)

Rehersal began on October 20, and the play opened on Broadway less than two months later. Reviews were poor, and the daunting competition from shows such as *Guys and Dolls, The King and I* and *South Pacific* also contributed to the closing of *See the Jaguar* after only five performances. The cast, which included Arthur Kennedy, a Tony Award winner for *Death of a Salesman*, were lauded for their game attempt in a losing effort, and Dean's notices were particularly positive. For the next year, he worked steadily in television dramas, playing variations of the tortured youth he portrayed in *See the Jaguar.*

## S 7    THE SCARECROW (Theatre de Lys, New York City, June 16, 1953. 6 performances.)

### Credits
Directed by Frank Corsaro; Written by Percy MacKaye, based on a story by Nathaniel Hawthorne; Produced by Terese Hayden; Music by Joseph Liebling; Scenery by William and Jean Eckart; Costumes by Ruth Morley

### Cast
Patricia Neal (Goody Rickby), Eli Wallach (Dickon), Anne Jackson (Rachel Merton), Milton Carney (Ebenezer), Bradford Dillman (Richard Talbot), Milton Selzer (Justice Gilead Merton), Douglas Watson (Lord Ravensbane), Mary Bell (Mistress Cynthia Merton), Albert Salmi (Captain Bugby), Alan MacAteer (Minister Dodge), Zita Rieth (Mistress Dodge), Harold Preston (Sir Charles Reddington), Sybil Baker (Mistress Reddington), Eavan O'Connor (Amelia Reddington), Ed Williams (Rev. Master Brand), Stefan Gierasch (Micah), JAMES DEAN

### Synopsis
In seventeenth-century Massachusetts, the devil tries to stir up trouble by bringing a scarecrow to life. The scarecrow takes the name of Lord Ravensbane, and is prepared to indulge his creator's whims, until he falls in love with Rachel Merton, a pretty New England maiden. Forced to choose between a life of servitude to the devil and his love for Rachel, Ravensbane chooses love. He dies, glad to have experienced a brief moment of joy as a human being.

### Reviews
"Concede to *The Scarecrow* the years that hang over its head. It is still an entertaining play with a sweeping style and a provocative theme. The performance is buoyant and gay." (*New York Times*, June 17, 1953)

### Commentary
*The Scarecrow* was written in 1908, and first staged on Broadway in 1911. The 1953 off-Broadway revival attracted a sterling cast, led by Patricia Neal, Eli Wallach and Anne Jackson. The director, Frank Corsaro, had met James Dean at the Actors Studio, and offered his friend a small role without dialogue in the play. Dean, who was between television jobs at the time, took the part. Douglas Watson, who played the lead role of Lord Ravensbane, was prepared to leave the show at one point, and Dean was offered to opportunity to take over the role. When Watson stayed, Dean left as soon as another television offer materialized.

## S 8   WOMEN OF TRACHIS (Cherry Lane Theatre, New York City, February 1954. 1 performance.)

### Commentary
The New School for Social Reserach presented a dramatic reading of *The Women of Trachis*, a one-act play by Sophocles adapted by Ezra Pound. For reasons that are unrecorded in all available sources, Dean was a participant in the reading, along with Eli Wallach and Joseph Sullivan. Howard Sackler directed, and Dean's friend Leonard Rosenman wrote the score.

## S 9   THE IMMORALIST (Previews in Philadelphia, and at The Royale Theatre in New York City, February 1, 1954. Opened at the Royale Theatre February 8, 1954. 104 performances.)

### Credits
Directed by Daniel Mann; Written by Ruth and Augustus Goetz, based on a novel by Andre` Gide; Produced by Billy Rose; Scenery by George Jenkins; Costumes by Motley; Lighting by Abe Feder

### Cast
Geraldine Page (Marcelline), John Heldabrand (Dr. Robert), Charles Dingle (Bocage), Louis Jourdan (Michel), JAMES DEAN (Bashir), Paul Huber (Dr. Garrin), David J. Stewart (Moktir), Adelaide Klein (Sidma), Bill Gunn (Dolit)

### Synopsis
Normandy, France, 1900--Michel, a handsome, young archaeologist, prepares to move to North Africa. At the age of 11, he was expelled from school after being found guilty of scandalous behavior with another boy, and he remains ostracized as an adult. Only Marcelline, "the most respected girl in the village," is upset that he is leaving, because she has loved him for years. At the last moment, she tells Michel of her feelings, and he marries her, hoping to free himself from the memory of his childhood indiscretion.

      The couple settle in Biskra, North Africa, a corrupt village rife with temptations for the repressed homosexual Michel. He has an affair with his houseboy, Bachir. Tormented by guilt, he renews his promise to be a good husband to Marcelline. After she becomes pregnant, Michel and Marcelline return to Normandy, aware of their mutual, lifelong confinement in a loveless marriage.

## Reviews
"James Dean makes a colorfully insinuating scapegrace." (*New York Herald Tribune*, February 9, 1954)

"It is beautifully produced and acted. . .Under Daniel Mann's direction, the performance is extraordinarily honest and skillful." (*New York Times*, February 9, 1954)

"It is James Dean as the houseboy who clearly and originally underlines the sleazy impertinence and the amoral opportunism which the husband must combat." (*New York World-Telegram and Sun*, February 9, 1954)

## Additional Reviews
*New York Daily Mirror* (February 9, 1954); *New York Daily News* (February 9, 1954); *New York Journal American* (February 9, 1954); *New York Post* (February 9, 1955); *Theatre Arts* (April 1954)

## Commentary
James Dean's most successful and significant stage credit was certainly *The Immoralist*; the play enjoyed a brief but prosperous Broadway run, and although Dean left the show after just fifteen performances, he won the Daniel Blum Award as the year's most promising personality, and it was his portrayal of Bashir that assured his casting in *East of Eden*.

The play was adapted from a 1902 semi-autobiographical novel by André Gide. James Dean auditioned for producer Billy Rose, and was cast in November of 1953. Cowriter Ruth Goetz remembered the audition in the documentary *Hollywood: The Rebel James Dean*; "He began to read and he was marvelous. He was instinctively, absolutely right. He had the quality of sweetness and charming attractiveness, and at the same time, a nasty undercurrent of suggestiveness and sexuality. And he was smashing." (see T-V1)

Rehersals began on December 18 at the Ziegfeld Theatre, during which time director Herman Shumlin was fired and replaced by Daniel Mann. Dean was upset about the change and was, according to Ruth Goetz, "abominable" in rehersal. The relationship may have been doomed from the start; when Dean once showed up a half-hour late for rehersal, Mann angrily asked him how long he had been in the theater. Dean glanced at his watch and said, "About four minutes."

During one particularly difficult day, after a harsh reprimand from Mann in front of the entire company, Dean stalked out of the theater. According to some sources, he tendered his resignation immediately after his opening-night performance, while others record Dean quitting two or three days later. Whichever is true, he gave his final performance on February 23. His dissatisfaction with the production was not the only cause of his early departure; Dean had already met with Elia Kazan, and was certain that his casting as Cal in *East of Eden* was imminent. He was replaced in the play by Phillip Pine.

The *Immoralist* was revived at New York City's Bouwerie Lane Theatre on November 7, 1963, and closed on May 10, 1964 after 210 performances. Richard Manuel played Dean's role of Bashir, opposite Frank Langella and Marcie Hubert as Michel and Marcelline. The play was directed by George Keathley and produced by Bruce Becker. The cast included Tom Klunis, Albert Ottenheimer, David Metcalf, Marian Carr, Cal Bellini, Paul Gennel and Russell Stagg.

# 4

# FILMOGRAPHY

**F1**  **FIXED BAYONETS** (20th Century-Fox, 1951; 92 minutes; black and white)

## Credits

Produced by Jules Buck; Directed and written by Samuel Fuller, based on a novel by John Brophy; Photography by Lucien Ballard; Music by Roy Webb; Edited by Nick De Maggio; Music directed by Lionel Newman; Art direction by Lyle Wheeler and George Patrick; Set direction by Thomas Little and Fred J. Rhode; Costumes by Charles Le Maire; Special effects by Fred Sersen; Techinical advisor, Captain Raymond Harvey

## Cast

Richard Basehart (Cpl. Denno), Gene Evans (Sgt. Rock), Michael O'Shea (Sgt. Lonergan), Richard Hylton (Wheeler), Craig Hill (Lt. Gibbs), Skip Homeier (Whitey), Henry Kulky (Vogl), Richard Monohan (Walowicz), Paul Richards (Ramirez), Tony Kent (Mainotes), Don Orlando (Borcellino), Patrick Fitzgibbon (Paddy), Neyle Morrow (Medic), George Wesley (Griff), Mel Pogue (Bulcheck), George Conrad (Zablocki), David Wolfson (Bigmouth), Buddy Thorpe (Husky Doggie), Al Negbo (Lean Doggie), Wyott Ordung (Fitz), Pat Hogan (Jonesy), JAMES DEAN (GI), John Doucette (GI), Bill Hickman, Kayne Shew

## Synopsis

Korea, 1951; a United States Army regiment, stationed on a remote mountaintop, is ordered to begin a strategic retreat. A small rear guard, under the command of Lt. Gibbs, is left behind to hold the line. Gibbs is killed in battle, as are the next two officers in the chain of command.

Corporal Denno, a quiet, sensitive soldier who has never fired his rifle at the enemy, is next in line. Fighting self-doubt and the incredulity of his men, Denno successfully completes the mission.

## Reviews

"Except in its general admiration for the tenacity and fortitude of men who suffer and die in a rugged, manly fashion, Mr. Fuller's latest film is lacking in any qualifications that might raise it above the routine." (*New York Times*, November 21, 1951)

"While the film may be technically solid, it leaves much to be desired...(it) remains a vivid picture of combat but does scant justice to the individual human dilemmas involved in the tragic scene." (*Newsweek*, December 3, 1951)

"Timeliness of the picture is its major asset, for the all-male cast has no one of top box office stature and the plot is merely a variation of themes often used in the past by other Hollywood war films." (*Variety*, November 21, 1951)

## Additional Reviews

*Christian Century* (January 2, 1952); *Commonweal* (December 14, 1951); *Film Daily* (November 26, 1951); *Holiday* (March 1952); *Hollywood Reporter* (November 21, 1951); *Library Journal* (January 1, 1952); *Motion Picture Herald Product Digest* (November 24, 1952); *The Nation* (January 5, 1952)

## Commentary

*Fixed Bayonets* is indeed James Dean's film debut, but his appearance is so brief that one almost has to take the reference books' word for it. Even the most dedicated Dean fan will have difficulty spotting him in a cast of identically-clad actors, whose mud and snow-covered features are further obscured by helmets and hooded jackets. The task was almost made easy--at one point during production Dean was given the line, "It's a rear guard coming back," but the line was cut before the film was released. However, it does provide a clue as to when he makes his appearance; at the ninety-minute mark, the surviving members of Corporal Denno's platoon are reunited with their regiment, and pass single-file through the center of the frame. James Dean is seventh in this solemn parade. His head bowed, his eyes blank, he is there and then gone in less than five seconds.

Apart from Dean's bit role, which he received as a favor from director Samuel Fuller to Dean's agent, Rogers Brackett, the only other unique quality of *Fixed Bayonets* is its release while the Allies, North

Koreans and Chinese were still conducting peace talks. There are some exciting moments, such as Denno's traversing through a minefield to rescue a fallen comrade, but the tension is undercut by an overdose of soldier-speak ("Should we send a regiment or a division? How about a platoon disguised as a division? Or a company at platoon-strength?"), and performances that vary from credible to superficial. All of the battles are studio-bound, but Fuller and cinematographer Lucien Ballard accomplish wonders with indoor sets.

**F2    SAILOR BEWARE** (Paramount, 1951; 108 minutes; black and white)

### Credits
Produced by Hal B. Wallis; Directed by Hal Walker; Written by James Allardice and Martin Rackin, with additional dialogue by John Grant, based on a play by Kenyon Nicholson; Adaptation by Elwood Ullman; Photography by Daniel L. Fapp; Edited by Warren Low; Music Directed by Joseph J. Lilley; Songs by Mack David and Jerry Livingston; Art direction by Hal Pereira and Henry Bumstead; Set direction by Sam Comer and Bertram Granger; Costumes by Edith Head; Sound recording by Harry Mills and Walter Oberst

### Cast
Dean Martin (Al Crowthers), Jerry Lewis (Melvin Jones), Corinne Calvet (Guest Star), Marion Marshall (Hilda Jones), Robert Strauss (Lardoski), Leif Erickson (Cdr. Lane), Don Wilson (Mr. Chubby), Vincent Edwards (Blayden), Skip Homeier (Mac), Dan Barton ('Bama), Mike Mahoney (Tiger), Mary Treen (Ginger), Betty Hutton (Betty), Dick Stabile (Band Leader), Donald MacBride (Chief Bos'n Mate), Louis Jean Heydt (Naval Doctor), Elaine Stewart (Lt. Saunders), Danny Arnold (Turk), Drew Cahill (Bill), James Flavin (Petty Officer), Dan Willis, JAMES DEAN (Sailors), Irene Martin, Mary Murphy (Pretty Girls), Darr Smith (Jeff Spencer), Bobby and Eddie Mayo (Themselves), Eddie Simms (Killer Jackson), Marshall Reed, John V. Close (Hospital Corpsmen), Jimmie Dundee (Bartender), Larry McGrath (Referee), The Marimba Merry Makers, Richard Karlan (Guard), Robert Carson (Naval Captain)

### Synopsis
Al Crowthers and Melvin Jones meet in line outside a New York City Navy recruitment office. Al has been there before--he pretends to join the service regularly to gain the admiration of patriotic lasses; Melvin plans to

sign up because his doctor recommended an ocean cruise to cure his allergies. Al, much to his chagrin, is accepted into the Navy, as is his strange new friend. They are assigned to a submarine, under the command of the gruff Petty Officer Ladroski. Various misadventures ensue, including an uproarious boxing match in which Melvin squares off against a powerful bruiser and manages to knock him out.

## Reviews
"Martin and Lewis are genial boys, and some of their knock-about clowning is in the classic tradition of good buffoons...(but) Lewis's characterization grows monotonous. Neither he nor the fellows who write for him have developed enough variety." (*New York Times*, February 1, 1952)

"Like their other movies, it will lay Martin & Lewis fans in the aisles, and leave other moviegoers mystified." (*Time*, February 18, 1952)

"While (the film) has been padded to an unnecessary 104 minutes, it has enough of the comics in hilarious routines to more than satisfy their considerable following. Less emphasis on plotting and more on Martin and Lewis would have made for better, overall comedy entertainment." (*Variety*, November 29, 1951)

## Additional  Reviews
*Christian Century* (April 9, 1952); *Film Daily* (November 29, 1951); *Holiday* (February 1952); *Hollywood Reporter* (November 29, 1951); *Motion Picture Herald Product Digest* (December 1, 1951); *Newsweek* (March 10, 1952)

## Commentary
*Sailor Beware* was the fifth feature film outing for the comedy team of Dean Martin and Jerry Lewis who, at the time, were the number two box-office attraction in the United States. The film was a very loose adaptation of the play *Sailor Beware!* that opened on Broadway on September 28, 1933. Horace MacMahon and George Heller played the lead roles of Mattie Matthews and Wop Wilchinski. On May 6, 1935, a new production opened in Harlem with an all-black cast, led by Carrington Lewis and Paul N. Johnson. The film adaptation changed all of the character names and large chunks of the plot, to accommodate the specialties of Martin and Lewis.

Some sources also cite the film as a remake of Paramount's *The Fleet's In*, a 1942 film starring Dorothy Lamour and William Holden, but the two stories bear only vague similarities. What little plot there is in *Sailor Beware* is designed only to set up a series of music and comedy routines that might have been lifted verbatim from the Martin and Lewis's nightclub act. The film's final thirty minutes ranks with the best work the duo achieved in motion pictures. A highlight is their boxing routine, in which Lewis brags about his fight against "Gene Tierney." "You mean Gene Tunney," responds Martin. "You fight who you want, I'll fight who I want," says Lewis, with all his trademark mugging and squealing.

It is during this scene, which appears approximately eighty minutes into the film, that James Dean makes his brief appearance. Dressed in a white t-shirt and slacks, he plays one of the corner men for Lewis's opponent in the boxing match. Overhearing Lewis's boasting in the locker room about his one hundred and one previous fights, Dean earnestly warns his fighter, "That guy's a professional!" It is his only line, but he can be spotted in the background throughout the locker room scene and the ensuing match.

## F3  HAS ANYBODY SEEN MY GAL? (Universal, 1952; 88 minutes; color)

### Credits
Produced by Ted Richmond; Directed by Douglas Sirk; Written by Joseph Hoffman, based on a story by Eleanor H. Porter; Photographed by Clifford Stine [Technicolor]; Music by Joseph Gershenson; Songs by Roy Smith, Roy Turk, Maceo Pinkard, Wendell Hall, Jelly Roll Morton, and Harry Woods; Edited by Russell Schoengarth; Art direction by Bernard Herzbrun and Hilyard Brown; Set decoration by Russell A. Gausman and John Austin; Costumes by Rosemary Odell. Choreography by Harold Belfer

### Cast
Piper Laurie (Millicent), Rock Hudson (Dan), Charles Coburn (Samuel Fulton), Gigi Perreau (Roberta), Lynn Bari (Harriet Blaisdell), Larry Gates (Charles Blaisdell), William Reynolds (Howard), Skip Homeier (Carl Pennock), Paul Harvey (Judge Wilkins), Frank Ferguson (Mr. Norton), Forrest Lewis (Martin Quinn), Gloria Holden (Mrs. Pennock), Fred Nurney (Fredericks), Sally Creighton (Arline Benson), Helen Wallace (Shirley White), Willard Waterman (Dr. Wallace); Fritz Feld (Alvarez), JAMES DEAN (Youth), Emory Parnell (Clancy), Charles Flynn (Joe), Barney Phillips (Workman), William Fawcett (Caretaker), Edna Holland (Seamstress), Leon Tyler (Personality Boy), Charles Williams (Reporter), Paul Bryar (Man), Joey Ray, Sam Pierce (Gamblers), Harmon Stevens (Real Estate Agent), Lyn Wilde (Charleston Dancer), Donna Leary (Charleston Dancer), Spec

O'Donnell (Candy Vendor), Larry Carr (Man), Earl Spainard, Eric Alden (Bits)

## Synopsis

Tarrytown, New York, in the late 1920's; Samuel Fulton, a wealthy, somewhat crotchety old millionaire, plans to leave his fortune to the Blaisdell family, the descendants of a girl who had spurned his marriage proposal decades earlier. Without the drive to prove himself that her refusal prompted, Fulton reasons, he might still be a $30-a-week clerk.

Curious to see what her family is like, he travels incognito to the small Vermont town where they live and, posing as a border, takes a room in the Blaisdell home. There, he sees history attempting to repeat itself; young Millie Blaisdell, the spitting image of her grandmother, is in love with Daniel, a soda jerk, but her mother urges her into a lucrative union with Carl Pennock, a wealthy but irresponsible snob. Fulton arranges for the family to receive $100,000 from an unnamed benefactor, to observe how their behavior would change when they receive his inheritance.

## Reviews

"There are folksy chuckles all along the way and the performances are gamely enthusiastic. But the film has been fashioned with such off-handed slickness that the average customer may rue his contribution at the box office." (*New York Times*, July 5, 1952)

"A thoroughly lightweight but agreeably lighthearted little taffy pull in Technicolor." (*Time*, July 28, 1952)

"A rather solid piece of nostalgic entertainment is offered in this comedy-drama of the '20's "flapper" era. It is beguiling, heartwarming fun for all and particularly for the family trade." (*Variety*, June 11, 1952)

## Additional Reviews

*BFI/Monthly Film Bulletin* (August 1952); *Film Daily* (June 11, 1952); *Hollywood Reporter* (June 6, 1952); *Library Journal* (November 1, 1952); *Motion Picture Herald Product Digest* (June 14, 1952); *Newsweek* (August 4, 1952)

## Commentary

The last and best of the films in which James Dean appeared before his ascent to stardom, *Has Anybody Seen My Gal?* contains the first scene in which Dean is allowed to speak a line of dialog from the foreground of the frame. In a drug store scene that begins about thirty minutes into the running time, he stands at the end of the counter, and says to Charles Coburn, "Hey, Gramps, I'll have a choc malt, heavy on the choc, plenty of milk, four spoons of malt, two scoops of vanilla ice cream, one mixed with the rest and one floating."

As with *Fixed Bayonets* and *Sailor Beware*, it was Dean's agent, Rogers Brackett, who helped him get the job. His one-scene appearance has no effect whatsoever on the caliber of the film. Piper Laurie and Rock Hudson are top-billed, but it is Charles Coburn's delightful performance as the Capra-esque curmudgeon Samuel Fuller that makes *Has Anybody Seen My Gal?* an engaging bit of froth. Hudson was launched to stardom in *Magnificent Obsession* (1954), one year before *East of Eden* did the same for James Dean. They did not get to   know each other well on the set of *Has Anybody Seen My Gal?*, but four years later they would work together again on *Giant*.

## F4    EAST OF EDEN (Warner Bros., 1955; 115 minutes; color)

Available on Videocassette and Laserdisc (Warner Bros.)

### Credits
Produced and directed by Elia Kazan; Written by Paul Osborn, based on the novel by John Steinbeck; Photographed by Ted McCord (CinemaScope, Warner Color), Music by Leonard Rosenman; Edited by Owen Marks; Art Direction by James Basevi and Malcolm Bert; Set Direction by George James Hopkins; Costumes by Anna Hill Johnstone; Sound by Stanley Jones; Dialogue Directed by Guy Thomajan; Makeup by Gordon Bau

### Cast
Julie Harris (Abra), JAMES DEAN (Cal Trask), Raymond Massey (Adam Trask), Richard Davalos (Aron Trask), Burl Ives (Sam), Jo Van Fleet (Kate), Albert Dekker (Will), Lois Smith (Ann), Harold Gordon (Mr. Albrecht), Timothy  Carey (Joe), Mario Siletti (Piscora), Lonny Chapman (Roy), Nick Dennis (Rantani)

### Synopsis
Monterey, California  in 1917: young Cal Trask follows a brothel owner back to her house of ill repute. He tries, unsuccessfully, to work up enough courage to speak to her, and then returns to his hometown of Salinas. Cal's father, Adam, reprimands him for staying out all night and wonders, not for the first time, why  the moody, troubled Cal can't be more like his dependable brother, Aron.

After a heated confrontation, Adam admits that Cal's mother is not really dead, as he had told his sons since their birth. Cal agrees to keep the secret from Aron, but he is now convinced that Kate, the

Monterey madam, is his mother. He goes back to see her and this time summons the courage to walk into her office, but she has him thrown out.

Despite his churlish behavior, Cal yearns for his father's approval, and tries to earn it by working feverishly on the family lettuce farm. After an experiment in refrigerating lettuce for long-distance travel proves a failure, Cal vows to recoup his father's financial losses. He asks his mother for $5000 to invest in a bean crop. Kate consents to the loan, relishing the irony of being able to help the estranged husband who thought her unfit to raise their sons. The price of beans soars after the United States enters World War I, and Cal reaps a substantial profit.

Cal falls in love with Aron's girlfriend, Abra. Together they plan a surprise birthday party for Adam, at which time Cal will give him the money as a gift. But when the moment comes, Adam refuses to accept the money, considering it tainted because it was made off the war. Devastated, Cal runs out of the house, where he is warned by his brother to stay away from Abra. Cal retaliates for this final affront by introducing Aron to his mother. Aron is shattered by the revelation; he gets drunk and joins the army. Adam has a stroke when he learns the news. Cal was ready to leave town as well, but chooses to stay behind with Abra and care for his father.

## Reviews

"For the stubborn fact is that the people who move about in this film are not sufficiently well established to give point to the anguish through which they go, and the demonstrations of their torment are perceptibly stylized and grotesque. Especially is this true of James Dean in the role of the confused and cranky Cal. This young actor, who is here doing his first big screen stint, is a mass of histrionic gingerbread." (*New York Times*, March 10, 1955)

"The picture is a brilliant entertainment and more than that, it announces a new star, James Dean, whose prospects look as bright as any young actor's since Marlon Brando...Dean tries so hard to find the part in himself that he often forgets to put himself into the part. But no matter what he is doing, he has the presence of a young lion and the same sense of danger about him. His eye is as empty as an animal's, and he lolls and gallops with the innocence and grace of an animal. Then, occasionally, he flicks a sly little look that seems to say, 'Well, all this is human, too--or had you forgotten?'" (*Time*, March 21, 1955)

"Much pro and con will develop about James Dean, unknown to whom Kazan gives a full-scale introduction. It is no credit to Kazan that Dean seems required to play his lead character as though he were straight out of a Marlon Brando mold. Just how flexible his talent is will have to be judged on future screen roles, although he has a basic appeal that manages to get through to the viewer despite the heavy burden of carboning another's acting style in voice and mannerisms. It should be interesting to see what he can do as Dean." (*Variety*, February 15, 1955)

## Additional Reviews
*America* (March 19, 1955); *An American Odyssey*, p.194-202; *Catholic World* (April 1955); *Commonweal* (March 11, 1955); *Elia Kazan: A Guide to References and Resources*, p.65-68; *Film Culture* (May-June 1955); *Film Daily* (February 16, 1955); *Films and Filming* (April 1955); *Films in Review* (March 1955); *Hollywood Reporter* (February 16, 1955); *Kazan on Kazan*, p.120-144; *Library Journal* (March 1, 1955); *The Nation* (April 2, 1955); *The New Republic* (April 25, 1955); *The New Yorker* (March 19, 1955); *Newsweek* (March 7, 1955); *Saturday Review* (March 19, 1955); *Sight and Sound* (Summer 1955); *Steinbeck on Film*, p. 137-151

## Commentary
*East of Eden* was the film that launched James Dean to stardom, and the only one of his three major films to be released when he was still alive.

Warner Bros. purchased the film rights to John Steinbeck's novel in November of 1952. Steinbeck was hired to write the script, for the unheard-of salary of $125,000 plus 25 percent of the film's net profits, but he pulled out early in the project, discouraged perhaps by the studio's intent to use only the final one-fourth of his novel. However, the author was very satisfied with the casting of Dean as Cal Trask. Director Elia Kazan introduced Dean to Steinbeck at Warners' New York office in February of 1954. "He *is* Cal!" was Steinbeck's elated verdict (see B059).

Just how Dean was cast in the role is still uncertain, as Kazan has told different stories to different sources. The most frequently-told anecdote is that Kazan attended a performance of *The Immoralist* in early 1954 (see S9), and then arranged a meeting with Dean a few days later. Some sources credit Paul Osborn, who assumed the scripting chores after Steinbeck's departure, with seeing Dean on stage and bringing him to Kazan's attention.

The studio announced Dean's casting on March 6, 1954. His forty-five page contract, dated April 7, 1954, paid him $1000 a week for ten weeks, with an option on a second film at $1250 a week, and a guaranteed weekly salary of $4000 should he make ten films for the studio. Dean spent part of his paycheck on a used Triumph T-110 motorcycle, which he drove at high speed around the back lot until Kazan pulled him over. "I don't care what you do to yourself when this film is in the can, but until then you are to stay off that thing." he ordered. (see B 045).

When Dean first showed up on the Warners lot, the film crew

thought he was a stand-in for the real star. Osborn's script was completed on May 17, and wardrobe tests began three days later. Kazan arranged for Dean to live with friends of assistant director Horace Hough in Salinas, where the actor could pick up the regional accents, gain a few pounds, and get a suntan. "Hopefully, he'll get some sleep," Kazan said. "You'd need two-by-fours to prop up the bags under his eyes. And get his hair cut." (see B044). Later, Kazan moved Dean into a $100 a month room across the street from the studio with Richard Davalos, who was cast as Aron. The director hoped the two young New York actors would forge a relationship that would lend an authentic chemistry to their scenes as antagonistic brothers.

Shooting began in Mendocino, California on May 27. Davalos had become fed up with Dean's unkempt habits and aloof manner, just as Kazan had wanted. Raymond Massey was likewise aggravated with Dean and his "Method actor" technique, which was indulged by the director. Dean was allowed whatever time he needed to prepare for a scene, and when he was ready Kazan would round up the other actors and commence filming. As with Davalos, the adversarial relationship between Massey and Dean was captured on film and proved beneficial to the finished product.

The scene that benefitted most from this discord was Adam's scolding of Cal at the dinner table, after Cal is forced to read from the Bible and does so with sarcastic disrespect. Kazan was not satisfied with the fervor of Massey's outburst, so he took Dean aside and instructed him to lace his recitation with a medley of profanity. When Dean did so, Massey thought that Dean, whom he already considered a young punk, had finally gone too far. Kazan used Massey's expression of fury in the film, and dubbed in the dialogue later.

After location work in Mendocino was complete, the balance of *East of Eden* was shot in Salinas, and on the Warners' back lot. On July 13, Marlon Brando visited the set; he had met Dean briefly, two years earlier, at the Actor's Studio in New York, and was playing Napoleon in *Desiree`* (1954) for 20th Century-Fox when he again shook the hand of the actor who would be compared to him in almost every *Eden* review. Dean was already familiar with the perception, it having shown up in reviews of his television work. In a letter he wrote to his friend Barbara Glenn while living in Salinas, he made light of the comparisons, signing his name "Jim (Brando Clift) Dean" (see B 045).

"(He) was throwing himself around, acting the madman," Brando later told Truman Capote. "So I spoke to him. I took him aside and asked him didn't he know he was sick? I gave him the name of an analyst and he went. And at least his work improved. Towards the end I think he was beginning to find his own way as an actor."

Dean's erratic behavior continued; he routinely showed up

exhausted, or late for work (on one occasion he stopped to watch Judy Garland shoot a dance sequence for *A Star is Born* [1954]), until Kazan again stepped in. "In desperation, Kazan fixed him up with a large dressing room on the lot," reported Look Magazine in 1956. The privilege, rarely granted, so delighted Dean that he never tired of it. At the end of filming *East of Eden*, he had to be all but evicted bodily to get him out of there. When informed that his dressing room was being commandeered for the use of a star in another production, he exclaimed, 'Holy smokes, I just remembered something.' "He raced back to his dressing room and pulled open his table drawer. It was stuffed with more than $5000 in small bills, representing salary that he had neglected to bank."

Before *East of Eden* premiered in New York on March 9, 1955, film industry screenings had produced a buzz about James Dean. Although many reviews mentioned the Brando comparison, sometimes unflatteringly, most agreed that Kazan had discovered a new star. "Dean is destined for a blazing career," wrote the *New York Daily Mirror*. The *Hollywood Reporter*'s assessment proved astonishingly prophetic; "He is that rare thing, a young actor who is a great actor, and the troubled eloquence with which he puts over the problems of misunderstood youth may lead to his being accepted by young audiences as a sort of symbol of their generation."

Reviews for other cast members were equally favorable. "They're all from the Actor's Studio," said Humphrey Bogart of the cast to reporter Joe Hyams. "Mumblers all. You'll need an interpreter to understand them." But Richard Davalos, Julie Harris and Jo Van Fleet (in her film debut) all achieve career high points in *East of Eden*. Van Fleet won the Academy Award for Best Supporting Actress, beating out Natalie Wood's performance in *Rebel Without a Cause*. Dean was nominated for Best Actor, but lost to Ernest Borgnine in *Marty*. The film also earned nominations for Best Director and Best Screenplay

It's the image of Dean from *Rebel Without a Cause* that has been marketed as his signature role, but it is *East of Eden* that contains James Dean's best motion picture performance. Credit belongs not just to Dean but to director Elia Kazan, who knew exactly how to motivate, and manipulate, the naturally gifted but undisciplined actor.

In the scene when Cal vents his rage in his father's ice house by hurling blocks of ice down a chute, Dean was unable to handle the blocks until Kazan made a derogatory remark about his acting. During the next take, Cal's anger surfaced through Jimmy's anger, and he lifted the blocks with ease. Later, after Dean sounded unconvincing in the scene when Cal speaks to Abra outside her window, Kazan got him drunk on Chianti. The idea worked.

The similarities between Dean's upbringing and that of Cal Trask

are obvious, and cannot be ignored in assessing his performance. The
loss of a mother at an early age, and the search to fill the void left by her
absence, was an emotional button that Kazan did not need to push. "Talk
to me, father!" Cal pleads early in the film, "I gotta know who I am! I gotta
know what I'm like!" Dean's searing portrayal in this scene, and his raw,
primal moan after Cal is rebuffed by Adam at the birthday party, have
resonated with alienated teenagers ever since.

"I chose him because he *is* Cal Trask," said Kazan in an on-set
interview with Joe Hyams. "He has a grudge against all fathers. He is
vengeful; he has a sense of aloneness and being persecuted. And he is
suspicious. In addition, he is tremendously talented." (see B045)

A musical stage adaptation of *East of Eden*, entitled *Here's
Where I Belong*, opened on March 3, 1968 at the Billy Rose Theatre in
New York, and closed after one performance. Produced by Mitch Miller in
association with United Artists, the musical was directed by Michael Kahn,
and written by Alex Gordon. The score, which included such songs as
"Cal Gets By," and "Raising Cain," was written by Robert Waldman and
Alfred Uhry. The cast included Paul Rogers as Adam Trask, Ken
Kercheval (later of TV's *Dallas*) as Aron, and Walter McGinn in Dean's role
of Cal. An original cast recording was released by United Artists Records.

In February of 1981, ABC television broadcast an eight-hour
remake of *East of Eden* in the form of a miniseries. The cast included
Jane Seymour as Kate, Timothy Bottoms as Adam, Sam Bottoms as Cal,
Lloyd Bridges as Sam Hamilton, and Bruce Boxleitner as Charles, Adam's
brother.

## F5  REBEL WITHOUT A CAUSE (Warner Bros., 1955; 111 minutes; color)
Available on Videocassette and Laserdisc (Warner Bros.)

### Credits
Produced by David Weisbart; Directed by Nicholas Ray; Written
by Stewart Stern, based on an adaptation by Irving Shulman of a
storyline by Ray, inspired from the story *The Blind Run* by Dr.
Robert M Lindner; Photographed by Ernest Haller
(CinemaScope, Warner Color); Music by Leonard Rosenman;
Edited by William Ziegler; Production designed by William
Wallace; Art direction by Malcolm Bert; Costumes by Moss Mabry;
Sound by Stanley Jones; Dialogue supervised by Dennis Stock;
Makeup by Gordon Bau

### Cast
JAMES DEAN (Jim Stark), Natalie Wood (Judy), Sal Mineo
(Plato), Jim Backus (Jim's Father), Ann Doran (Jim's Mother),

Corey Allen (Buzz), William Hopper (Judy's Father), Rochelle Hudson (Judy's Mother), Virginia Brissac (Jim's Grandma), Nick Adams (Moose), Jack Simmons (Cookie), Dennis Hopper (Goon), Marietta Canty (Plato's Maid), Jack Grinnage (Chick), Beverly Long (Helen), Steffi Sidney (Mil), Frank Mazzola (Crunch), Tom Bernard (Harry), Clifford Morris (Cliff), Ian Wolfe (Lecturer), Edward Platt (Ray), Robert Foulk (Gene), Jimmy Baird (Beau), Dick Wessel (Guide), Nelson Leigh (Sergeant), Dorothy Abbott (Nurse), Louise Lane (Woman Officer), House Peters (Officer), Gus Schilling (Attendant), Bruce Noonan (Monitor), Almira Sessions (Old Lady Teacher), Peter Miller (Hoodlum), Paul Bryar (Desk Sergeant), Paul Birch (Police Chief), Robert B. Williams (Moose's Father, Ed), David McMahon (Crunch's Father)

## Synopsis

Three troubled teenagers cross paths at a Los Angeles police station. Jim Stark is brought in on a drunk and disorderly charge, repeating the aberrant behavior that has already caused his parents to move several times. Judy, found wandering the streets after curfew, awaits with dread the arrival of her mother. Plato, a mentally disturbed rich kid, kills a litter of puppies for reasons he cannot explain to the arresting officer.

They meet again on the first day of high school; Jim asks Judy out on a date, but she rejects him and joins up with the leather-jacketed gang that is led by her boyfriend, Buzz. Plato warns Jim not to antagonize the gang, but during a field trip to the Griffith Observatory, Buzz goads Jim into a knife fight. Jim wins, but accepts another challenge from Buzz for a "chickie run" that night.

Just before the run the two combatants discover that they like each other. "Then why do we do this?" asks Jim. "You gotta do something," Buzz replies. Buzz is killed in the contest. Jim contemplates going to the police, but his parents talk him out of it. After attacking his father, Jim storms out of the house, picks up Judy and Plato, and together they explore a deserted mansion that has become Plato's secret retreat.

Buzz's gang thinks that Jim has confessed to the police, and track him down at the mansion. Plato pulls a gun and shoots one of the gang members. The police show up and Plato shoots at them as well, before taking refuge back in the Griffith Park Observatory. Judy and Jim follow him inside. After a tense stand-off, Jim convinces Plato to turn himself in. But when the unbalanced youth sees the gathering of police outside the observatory, he panics and runs, and is killed by an officer's gun.

48 James Dean

## Reviews
"Convincing or not in motivations, this tale of tempestuous kids and their weird ways of conducting their social relations is tense with explosive incidents...However, we do wish the young actors, including Mr. Dean, had not been so intent on imitating Marlon Brando in varying degrees. The tendency, possibly typical of the behavior of certain youths, may therefore be a subtle commentary but it grows monotonous." (*New York Times*, October 27, 1955)

"The late James Dean reveals completely the talent latent in his *East of Eden* performance. As a new and unwilling member of the gang, a boy who recognized more clearly than any of the others his need for help, he projects the wildness, the torment and the crude tenderness of a restless generation. Gone are the Brando mannerisms, gone too the obvious Kazan touch. He stands as a remarkable talent; and he was cut down, it would seem, by the very passions he exposes so tellingly in this strange and forceful picture." (*Saturday Review*, October 1955)

"Here is a fairly exciting, suspenseful and provocative, if also occasionally far-fetched, melodrama of unhappy youth on another delinquency kick. ...the performance of the star, James Dean, will excite discussion, especially in connection with the irony of his own recent crash death under real-life conditions of recklessness which form a macabre pressagent fame as the picture goes into release. ..Dean is very effective as a boy groping for adjustment to people. As a 'farewell' performance he leaves behind, with this film, genuine artistic regret, for here was a talent which might have touched the heights. His actor's capacity to get inside the skin of youthful pain, torment and bewilderment is not often encountered." (*Variety*, October 14, 1955)

## Additional Reviews
*America* (November 5, 1955); *BFI/Monthly Film Bulletin* (January 1956); *Commonweal* (November 11, 1955); *Diacritics* (1980); *Esquire* (October 1982); *Film Culture* (1956); *Film Daily* (October 27, 1955); *Film Quarterly* (1974); *Films and Filming* (August 1977); *Films Illustrated* (June 1976); *Films in Review* (November 1955); *Hollywood Reporter* (October 21, 1955); *Motion Picture Herald Product Digest* (October 22, 1955); *The Nation* (December 3, 1955); *The New Republic* (March 6, 1976); *The New Yorker* (November 5, 1955); *Newsweek* (November 7, 1955); *Rolling Stone* (June 20, 1974); *Sight and Sound* (Fall 1956); *Take One* (1979); *Time* (November 28, 1955)

## Commentary
*Rebel Without a Cause* was a 1944 book about juvenile delinquency by

Dr. Robert Linder. Warner Bros. purchased the movie rights to the book in 1946, intending it as a vehicle for Marlon Brando. When Brando opted to remain on the New York stage, *Rebel* was cast into the canceled projects file, where it remained for the next eight years.

In 1954, after Columbia Pictures had a hit with *The Wild One*, and while MGM was shooting *The Blackboard Jungle*, Warners resurrected *Rebel*, and Nicholas Ray was hired to direct. Ray immediately began making changes in the story, and then discarded it completely in favor of a 17-page treatment entitled *The Blind Run*, that he completed on September 18, 1954. The studio agreed that Ray's story was better than Dr. Robert Linder's, but rejected the title in favor of the original. Irving Shulman was hired to transform Ray's treatment into a script, replacing Leon Uris. Shulman completed an adaptation, but he, too, was ultimately replaced in favor of Stewart Stern, who is the screenwriter of record.

Once the script was finished, it was submitted to the studio censor. Among the many changes made during this stop was any implication that Judy, the character played by Natalie Wood, was sexually promiscuous. Originally, she first appeared in the police station after being arrested for solicitation. The love scene between Jim Stark and Judy was trimmed, the word "punk" was removed, and an attempt was made, albeit unsuccessfully, to tone down the suggestion of homosexual affection between Jim and Plato.

James Dean signed on to the project in December of 1954, but not without some concern over its glorified 'B' movie heritage. After becoming a star in a film adaptation of a John Steinbeck novel, his participation in a project with an unproven script and director might be perceived as a backward step. It was Nicholas Ray who, after being mesmerized by Dean at an industry screening of *East of Eden*, convinced the actor that there was powerful potential in the material.

The first script reading was conducted at the Chateau Marmont Hotel in Los Angeles. Also present was fifteen year-old Sal Mineo and seventeen year-old Natalie Wood, whose affair with the 44 year-old Ray has been cited as the reason for her casting over Margaret O'Brien and Debbie Reynolds. *Rebel* thus became one of a select few movies about teenagers to cast actual teenagers in lead roles.

To prepare for the film, James Dean spent two weeks visiting Los Angeles neighborhoods that were frequented by youth gangs. He also read, as did other cast members, the chapter "Creation of a Delinquent Character" from a book entitled *Delinquents in the Making*. Wardrobe tests began on March 23, and five days later shooting began at Griffith Park.

Within a week, production was halted by order of studio chief Jack Warner. On March 16, *East of Eden* had opened in Los Angeles, and James Dean was being touted as a major new star. Warner realized that Dean's next project now had enormous box-office potential, and acted accordingly. The film would be shot in color, instead of black and white as originally planned. As a result, Ray replaced the black leather jacket worn by Jim Stark with the red nylon windbreaker that now ranks with Charlie Chaplin's bowler hat and Humphrey Bogart's trenchcoat in the annals of legendary cinema costumes.

The film's budget was increased, and the shooting schedule was extended, which allowed Warners' new star the time he required to prepare for every scene. Jim Backus, who played Dean's father, wrote in his autobiography *Rocks on the Roof* about one particularly memorable example of Dean's technique; "The scene called for him to have an intensely dramatic argument with the (police) officer in charge, and end up by hysterically banging on the desk in frustration and rage. He kept the cast and crew waiting for one whole hour...(while) sitting in his darkened dressing room with a record player blasting out *Ride of the Valkyrie*, and drinking a quart of cheap red wine.

"When he felt ready, he stormed out, strode onto the set, did the scene, which was practically a seven-minute monologue, *in one take*, so brilliantly, that even the hard-boiled crew cheered and applauded." (see B007). This scene also brought Jimmy's Method training to the fore--he punched the desk so hard that he had to be rushed to the hospital. No bones were broken, but his hand was bandaged for a week.

Dean was injured again while shooting the knife-fight sequence with Corey Allen, who played the doomed Buzz. Allen unintentionally nicked Dean's ear, causing a trickle of blood to flow down the right side of his face. Ray stopped the scene and called for a first aid man, which infuriated Dean. "Can't you see this is a real moment?" he yelled to the director. "Don't you ever cut a scene while I'm having a real moment. That's what I'm here for." (see B045)

Several lines and scenes were changed slightly from the script by Ray and by Dean, who was given considerable freedom to improvise. The entire opening sequence of *Rebel*, in which Jim Stark rolls around on a residential street, playing with a toy monkey, was made up by Dean on the spot. "It wasn't even rehearsed," recalled costar Beverly Long. "And I remember sitting there and just being blown away. I remember thinking, 'Oh, my God. I'm working with a genius. He's crazy, but he's really, really talented.'" (see B109)

*Rebel Without a Cause* wrapped production on May 26, 1955, three days after shooting commenced on Dean's next and last film, *Giant*. *Rebel* opened in New York's Astor Theater on October 26, 1955, less than four weeks after Dean's death. Warner Bros. was concerned that his demise might have a negative impact on the box-office, but after several hastily-called meetings it was decided to release the film on schedule and with the original marketing campaign, which was built entirely around

James Dean.

It's impossible to gauge with any certainty the effect Dean's death ultimately had on *Rebel*'s gross of $8 million, which was enough to make the film a respectable hit. It is fascinating to speculate whether the movie would have performed as well had Dean survived. The film earned Academy Award nominations for Sal Mineo (Best Supporting Actor), Natalie Wood (Best Supporting Actress) and Best Screenplay.

Contemporary reviews raved that Dean fulfilled the promise he showed in *East of Eden*, but by any criteria *Rebel Without a Cause* is inferior to its predecessor. The unfocused script shows all the evidence of having passed through several writers and several versions. Jim's parents, and Judy's parents, are more like cartoons than three-dimensional chracters. Mr. Stark (Jim Backus) is particularly ridiculous, though the fault for this lies in the script, not in Backus's performance. And despite the studio's 'A' picture treatment, *Rebel* cannot completely hide its status as the type of juvenile delinquency melodrama that Roger Corman turned out every two weeks in the late 1950s and early 1960s.

Nicholas Ray's kinetic direction, and the performances of James Dean, Natalie Wood and Sal Mineo are responsible for elevating the material well beyond what was actually there. Dean's most riveting moment comes in the opening scene, when Jim unburdens himself to a friendly police captain (Edward Platt). "If I had one day when I didn't have to be all confused," he cries, "when I felt that I belonged someplace." Like Cal in *East of Eden*, Jim's isolation struck a chord with millions of troubled adolescents. "His bewilderment at being rejected by the high school gang came through the camera with an anguish that projected itself beyond the screen and became the aching hurt of every kid who had ever been hit on the nose," wrote *Look* magazine in 1956.

Although Dean did not live to see the impact of his performance, he did attend a preview screening shortly before his death. According to *Look* magazine, he was "unnerved" by his acting, and by the audience reaction. "He slipped out of the theater to sit in a car parked down the street. But afterward, he asked a friend, 'How'd I do? How was I?'"

## F6 GIANT (Warner Bros., 1956; 201 minutes; color)

Available on Videocassette and Laserdisc (Warner Bros.)

### Credits
Produced by George Stevens and Henry Ginsberg; Directed by George Stevens; Written by Fred Guiol and Ivan Moffat, based on the novel by Edna Ferber; Photographed by William C. Mellor (Warner Color); Music by Dmitri Tiomkin, song by Tiomkin and Paul Francis Webster; Edited by William Hornbeck, Fred

Bohanan and Phil Anderson; Production designed by Boris
Leven and Ralph Hurst; Costumes by Marjorie Best and Moss
Mabry; Sound by Earl Gain; Makeup by Gordon Bau

## Cast
Elizabeth Taylor (Leslie Benedict), Rock Hudson (Bick Benedict),
JAMES DEAN (Jett Rink), Carroll Baker (Luz Benedict II), Jane
Withers (Vashti Snythe), Chill Wills (Uncle Bawley), Mercedes
McCambridge (Luz Benedict), Sal Mineo (Angel Obregon III),
Dennis Hopper (Jordan Benedict III), Judith Evelyn (Mrs. Horace
Lynnton), Paul Fix (Dr. Horace Lynnton), Rod Taylor (Sir David
Karfrey), Earl Holliman (Bob Dace), Robert Nichols (Pinky
Smythe), Alexander Scourby (Old Polo), Fran Bennett (Judy
Benedict), Charlie Watts (Whiteside), Elsa Cardenas (Juana),
Carolyn Craig (Lacey Lynnton), Monte Hale (Bale Clinch), Mary
Ann Edwards (Adarene Clinch), Sheb Wooley (Gabe Target),
Victor Millan (Angel Obregon I), Mickey Simpson (Sarge), Pilar de
Rey (Mrs. Obregon), Maruice Jara (Dr. Guerra), Noreen Nash
(Lorna Lane), Napoleon Whiting (Swazey), Tina Menard (Lupe),
Ray Whitley (Watts), Felipe Turich (Gomez), Francisco Villalobos
(Mexican Priest), Ana Maria Majaica (Petra), Guy Teague (Harper),
Nativadid Vacio (Eusebio), Max Terhune (Dr. Walker), Ray
Bennett (Dr. Borneholm), Barbara Barrie (Mary Lou Decker),
George Dunne (Verne Decker), Slim Talbot (Clay Hodgins), Tex
Driscoll (Clay Hodgins, Sr.), Juney Ellis (Essie Lou Hodgins),
Charles Meredith (Minister), Rush Williams (Waiter), Bill Hale
(Bartender), Tom Monroe, Mark Hamilton (Guards), John Wiley
(Assistant Manager), Ina Poindexter (Young Woman), Carl Moore
(Toastmaster), Ella Ethridge (General's Wife), Paul Kruger
(General), Eddie Baker (Governor), Ethel Greenwood
(Governor's Wife), Fernando Alvarado, Tony Morella (Busboys),
Julian Rivero (Old Man), Maxine Gates (Mrs. Sarge), Richard and
David Bishop (Jordan as an Infant), Steven Kay (Jordan at Age 4),
Mary Ann and Georgann Cashen (Judy as an Infant), Christine
Werner (Luz as an Infant), Judy and Jill Lent (Luz at Age 2), John
Garcia (Angel as an Infant), David Jiminez (Angel at Age 5),
Colleen and Marlene Crane (Judy II as an Infant), Wanda Lee
Thompson (Judy II at Age 2), Perfideo Aguilar and Margaret
Trujillo (Jordy IV as an Infant), Ramon Ramirez (Jordan IV at Age
2)

## Synopsis
Wealthy Texan Bick Benedict brings his new wife, Leslie, home to his
massive half-million acre ranch, Reata. Leslie finds the transition difficult at

first; she is shocked at the poor medical treatment received by Reata's Mexican ranch hands, and by her husband's antiquated outlook on a woman's place in marriage. Bick's sister, Luz, is resentful of Leslie's intrusion into the family, and heightens Leslie's uneasiness.

Luz is killed after she is thrown from a wild horse. In her will, she leaves a small portion of Reata to Jett Rink, a surly ranch hand who is jealous of Bick's wealth, and of his marriage to Leslie. Bick offers Jett double what the land is worth to sell, but Jett opts instead to dig for oil. His gamble pays off--Jett hits a gusher, and uses the profits to buy other land and sink other wells. Eventually, his oil empire rivals Bick's cattle kingdom in prominence and profits.

Oil fever sweeps Texas, but Bick stubbornly refuses to blemish Reata's beautiful open spaces with ugly derricks. His neighbors have no such qualms, and most of them sell out to Jett. Bick's oldest son, Jordan, comes of age to take over his father's position, but chooses instead to become a doctor. Even more disheartening to Bick is the affair between his daughter, Luz II, and Jett.

The animosity between Jett Rink and the Benedicts boils over at a banquet held to honor Jett. Blows are exchanged between Jordan and Jett, and when Bick later tries to attack his old nemesis, he finds Jett so drunk that he can only walk away in disgust. Jett, a bitter, lonely man despite his immense wealth, confesses to Luz that the only woman he ever loved was Leslie, and at one point he attempted unsuccessfully to make her his mistress.

On the way back to Reata, Bick is outraged at a diner owner's refusal to serve a Mexican family. An argument ensues that ends in a fight. Bick is soundly beaten, but he wins anew the love and respect of his family.

## Reviews

"Thanks to Mr. Stevens' brilliant structure and handling of images, every scene and every moment is a pleasure. However, it is the late James Dean who makes the malignant role of the surly ranch hand who becomes an oil baron the most tangy and corrosive in the film. Mr. Dean plays this curious villain with a stylized spookiness--a sly sort of off-beat languor and slur of language--that concentrates spite. This is a haunting capstone to the brief career of Mr. Dean." (*New York Times*, October 11, 1956)

"James Dean, who was killed in a sports car crash two weeks after his last scene in *Giant* was shot, in this film clearly shows for the first (and fatefully the last) time what his admirers said he had: a streak of genius. He has caught the Texas accent to nasal perfection, and mastered the lock-hipped, high-heeled, stagger of the wrangler, and wry little jerks and smirks, tics and twitches, grunts and giggles that make up most of the language of a man who talks to himself a good deal more than he talks to anyone else." (*Time*, October 22, 1956)

"An excellent film which registers strongly on all levels...In the light of the current death cult starring the late James Dean it's probably safe to assume that he'll be the strongest draw on the marquee. No one should be disappointed, and the film only proves what a promising talent has been lost. As the shiftless, envious, bitter ranch hand who hates society, Dean delivers an outstanding portrayal." (*Variety*, October 10, 1956)

## Additional  Reviews
*Commonweal* (October 26, 1956); *Film Culture* (1956); *Film Daily* (October 10, 1956); *Films and Filming* (February 1957); *Films in Review* (November 1956); *Hollywood Reporter* (October 10, 1956); *Movie* (November 1962); *The Nation* (October 20, 1956); *The New Yorker* (October 20, 1956); *Newsweek* (October 22, 1956); *Saturday Review* (October 13, 1956); *Sight and Sound* (Winter 1956)

## Commentary
In her 1952 novel *Giant*, Edna Ferber described the character of Jett Rink as "all right when he behaves himself. When he drinks he goes kind of crazy. He's a kind of genius, Jett is. He's got a grudge against the world. He'll probably end up a billionaire--or in the electric chair. Put him in a car and he goes crazy."

When the film went into preproduction in 1953, three years before its eventual release, the studio's list of contenders for the role of Jett included such disparate names as Marlon Brando and Charleton Heston, Montgomery Clift and Robert Mitchum, Richard Burton and Cornel Wilde.

James Dean read an early version of the *Giant* script before he was cast in *East of Eden*, and thought himself perfect for the role of Jett. It was only after *Eden* was released to glowing reviews did anyone at Warner Bros. agree with him. Ferber never did. She had admired Dean in *East of Eden*, and known of him since attending a performance of *The Immoralist* on Broadway, but thought he was miscast.

Director George Stevens was cajoled with compliments from James Dean for months before he was offered the role. "George Stevens, for my money, is the greatest director of them all--even greater than Kazan," said Dean according to a Warner Bros. press release; "This Stevens was born for the movies. He's so real, so unassuming, and he doesn't miss a thing. You know, when it wants to, Hollywood can accomplish tremendous things. And this movie might be one of them. I sure hope so."

However, after *Giant* went into production on May 23, 1955 (three days before Dean finished work on *Rebel Without a Cause*), the relationship between actor and director rapidly deteriorated. Dean joined the cast in Marfa, Texas on June 3, and astonished the cast, crew and assorted onlookers by urinating on the ground, then returning to the set and announcing to Stevens, "Okay, let's go. I'm ready." Dean told his friend and costar Dennis Hopper that he did it to calm his nerves on the first day of shooting; "If I could [do that] in front of all those people, and be cool about it, I could go in front of the camera and do just about anything at all," he reasoned. However, Stevens could not be blamed for interpreting Dean's behavior as a show of defiance, the symbolic act of "marking his territory," or at the very least, a deed of disrespect. It was not an auspicious beginning, and it would get worse.

Dean came to the set with his own vision of the film and of his role, and was used to having his ideas regarded on the set. Stevens, however, had been directing motion pictures since the days of the silents, and figured he already knew how to make a movie. When he told Dean how to play a scene, he expected obedience, not suggested alternatives.

As Randall Riese correctly observed in *The Unabridged James Dean*, *Giant* was the young actor's first "purely Hollywood picture," and Stevens was in many ways the ultimate Hollywood director; "*East of Eden* may have been filmed on the West Coast, but its mentality, its attitude, its soul, its director, and its actors were decidedly East Coast. On *Rebel Without a Cause*, Nicholas Ray directed the production as he did all of his pictures--independently, as distanced from the Hollywood realm as he could possibly be.

"(Stevens') approach to *Giant*...was to shoot every scene from virtually every angle and then to conjure up some magic in the editing room," Riese writes. "Kazan had a tremendous talent for working with actors. Stevens, a visualist, was not an actor's director." Stevens' impatience with improvisation, his emphasis on the technical over the creative, and on the big picture over the intimate moment, were anathema to the Method-trained Dean.

On August 1, Stevens compiled a list of the shooting delays caused by James Dean. There are sixteen entries, ranging in length from fifteen minutes to a full day. To say that the production had by this point split into two camps, Dean's and Stevens', is accurate but misleading, since Dean's camp was severely outnumbered. His only friends on the set were Elizabeth Taylor, to whom he would confide his misgivings in frequent late-night phone conversations, Mercedes McCambridge, and dialogue director Bob Hinkle, who taught Dean the rope tricks that he used in the film to steal scenes from Rock Hudson.

The enthusiastic advance word about *Rebel Without a Cause*

allowed Dean's agent, Jane Deacy, to negotiate a new contract for her client, which raised his salary from $1500 a week to $100,000 a picture. Dean had already started boxing lessons to prepare for his role as Rocky Marciano in *Somebody Up There Likes Me* (see W9).

On September 17, Dean completed his last day of shooting on *Giant*. On September 19, he test-drove a silver Porsche 550 Spyder at Competition Motors, on North Vine Street in Hollywood. He purchased the car on September 21. Nine days later, while Rock Hudson and Elizabeth Taylor filmed several scenes in the interior of the Benedict mansion, Reata, Dean was killed in a collision at the corner of U.S. 466 and Highway 41. That night, while Taylor, Stevens, Carroll Baker and others watched the results of the day's shooting, news of Dean's death reached the projection room via telephone.

Filming continued the following day, though Elizabeth Taylor arrived three hours late and was visibly shaken throughout the afternoon. She left early, and was hospitalized the following week due to an emotional breakdown. On October 12, after 115 shooting days, *Giant* officially completed production, 37 days late and $5.4 million over budget. It was later discovered that the banquet speech delivered by a drunk Jett Rink was inaudible due to technical sound problems. Nick Adams, a friend of Dean's who appeared in *Rebel Without a Cause*, dubbed the speech with wads of gum in his cheeks.

*Giant* was not released until October 10, 1956, just over one year after the death of James Dean. For months, Stevens supervised editing on the film while under siege from the dawning Dean cult. Fans knew that *Giant* contained the last new footage they would ever see of their idol, and wrote letters threatening drastic reprisals if just one frame of Dean was removed from the final cut.

Stevens remained true to his personal vision of the film when he was challenged on the set by Dean, and was not about to be swayed by the actor's fans. The movie was cut to his specifications, and released to rave reviews. *Giant* became the third highest-grossing film of 1956, the only one of James Dean's films to reach the top ten, and received ten Academy Award nominations; Best Picture, Best Actor (Rock Hudson), Best Actor (James Dean), Best Supporting Actress (Mercedes McCambridge), Best Screenplay, Best Art Direction, Best Costume Design, Best Editing and Best Score. Only George Stevens won the Oscar.

It is hard to argue with the Academy's judgment. *Giant* is George Stevens' film; his imprint is more perceptible than any individual contributions from the cast. The amazing visuals he framed and shot from every angle are what remain most indelible; a dark, Gothic mansion standing in the middle of a vast, desolate landscape, the famous image of Dean, his cowboy hat pulled down low over his forehead, seated behind the wheel of a vintage roadster. Very few films need to run over 200 minutes, and *Giant* is not one of them, but every few minutes Stevens caught something magnificent in his cameras that held the viewer's eye and attention through the often prolonged lapses in narrative.

The performances, however, are not without merit. *Giant* is Rock Hudson's best film, Carroll Baker's best after *Baby Doll* (1956), one of Elizabeth Taylor's best (for some reason all her choice work is done in movies that put her on horseback), and is among the better credits on the resumes` of Dennis Hopper, Rod Taylor and Jane Withers. Mercedes McCambridge received a Best Supporting Actress nomination for a performance that barely lasted fifteen minutes.

The most challenging role, and the most interesting, belonged to James Dean. The charter of Jett Rink aged from 19 to 47, but remained an insecure child throughout. Blinded by jealousy, lust and greed, Rink was, in the words of Randall Riese, "American capitalism at its ugliest." Although the makeup job used to mature Dean into middle-age is not convincing, his portrayal of Jett as a bitter, broken man is superb. "In one scene," raved *Time* magazine, "in a long drunken mumble with Carroll Baker, Dean is able to press an amazing array of subtleties into the mood of the movement, to achieve what is certainly the finest piece of atmospheric acting seen on the screen since Marlon Brando and Rod Steiger did their 'brother' scene in *On the Waterfront.*"

It would be hard to imagine two actors further apart on any basis of comparison than Rock Hudson and James Dean. Hudson, tall and broad-shouldered, had the clean-cut handsome features and confident manner of a classic matinee idol. Dean, with his slight build, angular face and unkempt hair, projected discomfort and turmoil with every wavering movement. Dean was the tortured genius, whose disruptive behavior was tolerated because of his genuine gift for the acting craft; Hudson was the reliable company man, always on time, always prepared, proficient but rarely prodigious.

Not surprisingly, Hudson and Dean did not bond on the set, and their mutual disrespect no doubt increased the tension between the characters they played. The discord of their acting styles was not a detriment to the film. However, Dean's best scenes were those opposite Elizabeth Taylor, whose sympathetic attitude toward Dean was echoed in Leslie's unlikely friendship with Jett Rink. "You're an odd one, Jett. But I like you," Leslie says to Jett early in the film, a line that Taylor might have spoke to Dean when the cameras stopped.

In the early 1980s, producer Gene Taft purchased the rights for *Giant, Part II: Reata* from the estate of Edna Ferber. The project, which never went before the cameras, was to have been scripted by Robert Garland, and was touted as including never-before-seen footage of Dean from *Giant.*

James Dean as Jim Stark in *Rebel Without a Cause*, 1955. (Photograph courtesy of Photofest)

# 5

# RADIO/TELEVISION

## Radio

**R 1    Alias Jane Doe**
**Hallmark Playhouse,**
**Stars Over Hollywood,**
**The Theatre Guild of the Air** (CBS-Radio 1950-1951)

In the early 1950s, Rogers Brackett, who at that time was James Dean's agent, worked for the advertising agency Foote, Cone and Belding. Brackett helped Dean receive bit parts on several radio drama sponsored by the agency.

## Television

**T 1    Commercial** (all networks-TV); 1950; black and white

On December 13, 1950, nineteen-year-old James Dean was paid ten dollars and a boxed lunch to appear in a commercial for Pepsi-Cola. It was his first professional acting job. The commercial was shot at Griffith Park in Los Angeles, California. He had no lines, but was part of a small group of teenagers who sang the then-current Pepsi jingle. Nick Adams and Beverly Long, both of whom appear in *Rebel Without a Cause*, were also cast.

**T 2    Family Theatre** (syndicated-TV) March 25, 1951; 60 minutes; black and white

**Credits**
Directed by Arthur Pierson; Produced by Patrick Peyton;

**Cast**
Ruth Hussey, Joan Leslie, Gene Lockhart, Jeanne Cagney, Leif Erickson, Regis Toomey, Henry Brandon, Nelson Leigh, Gordon Oliver, Roddy McDowall, Frank Wilcox, Everett Glass, Charles Meredith, Michael Ansara, JAMES DEAN

*Family Theatre*, also known as *Father Peyton's TV Theatre*, was a series of religous specials produced for television by Father Patrick Peyton and Jerry Fairbanks. "Hill Number One" was presented on Easter Sunday, 1951. The story attempted to from an analogy between the events leading to the crucifixion and resurrection of Jesus Christ, and the struggle of a platoon of American soldiers ordered to recapture a hill during the Korean War. James Dean, in his dramatic television debut, had the small role of John the Apostle.

**T 3      The Web** (CBS-TV) February 20, 1952; 30 minutes; black and white

**Credits**
Directed by Lela Swift; Produced by Franklin Heller; Hosted and narrated by Jonathan Blake

**Cast**
Anne Jackson, E.G. Marshall, Robert Simon, JAMES DEAN

*The Web* was a popular anthology series that broadcast adaptations of stories written by members of the Mystery Writers of America. James Dean appeared as a bellhop who helps solve a murder in an episode entitled "Sleeping Dogs."

**T 4      Studio One** (CBS-TV) March 3, 1952; 60 minutes; black and white

**Credits**
Directed by Paul Nickell; Written and produced by Worthington Minor, based on a story by Robert Carson

**Cast**
John Forsythe, Catherine McLeod, Vaughn Taylor, Joe Morass, JAMES DEAN

The first of Dean's three appearances on *Studio One* has him cast once again as a bellhop (see T3), in an episode entitled "Ten Thousand Horses Singing."

**T5    Lux Video Theatre** (CBS-TV) March 17, 1952; 30 minutes; black and white

**Credits**
Directed by  Richard Goode; Written by J. Albert Hirsch; Produced by Cal Kuhl

**Cast**
James Barton, Muriel Kirkland, Richard Bishop, JAMES DEAN

After sixteen successful years on radio, *Lux Radio Theatre* became *Lux Video Theatre* in 1950.  James Dean costarred in a story entitled "The Foggy, Foggy  Dew."

**T6    Kraft Television Theatre** (NBC-TV) May 21, 1952; 30 minutes; black and white

**Credits**
Written by E.P. Conkle

**Cast**
Thomas Coley (Abraham Lincoln), Pat Breslin, Una O'Connor, William Lee, Butch Clavell, JAMES DEAN

A fictional drama about an episode in the life of young Abraham Lincoln, entitled "Prologue to Glory," contained the first of James Dean's three appearances on *Kraft Television Theatre*.

**T7    Studio One** (CBS-TV) May 26, 1952; 60 minutes; black and white

**Credits**
Written by John Drinkwater

**Cast**
Robert Pastene (Abraham Lincoln), JAMES DEAN (WILLIAM SCOTT)

Dean plays a soldier from Vermont who is court-martialed for falling asleep during guard duty in "Abraham Lincoln." The soldier is later pardoned by Abraham Lincoln.

**T8    Hallmark Hall of Fame** (NBC-TV) June 2, 1952; 60 minutes; black and white

### Credits

### Cast
Cloris Leachman, Don McHenry, Nancy Malone, JAMES DEAN

In "Forgotten Children," Dean plays a Southern aristocrat.

**T9    The Kate Smith Show** (NBC-TV) January 15, 1953; 60 minutes; black and white

### Credits
Written by Earl Hamner, Jr.

### Cast
John Carradine, JAMES DEAN (ANGEL), Edgar Stehli

Kate Smith's popular variety series ran for four years on NBC's daytime schedule. In the dramatic presentation "Hound of Heaven," Dean played an angel.  The writer, Earl Hamner Jr., would later created the popular television series *The Waltons.*

**T10    Treasury Men in Action** (NBC-TV) January 29, 1953; 30 minutes; black and white

A crime drama that based its stories on actual cases from the files of the U.S. Treasury Department. Walter Greaza, the only series regular, played the chief investigator. Dean played a supporting role in an episode entitled "The Case of the Watchful Dog."

**T11    You Are There** (CBS-TV) February 8, 1953; 30 minutes; black and white

Walter Cronkite hosted this series, which presented reenactments of historical events, as they would be covered by broadcast news correspondents. On his twenty-second birthday, James Dean costarred in "The Capture of Jesse James" as Bob Ford, the man who killed the infamous outlaw. The episode was directed by Sidney Lumet.

**T12  Danger** (CBS-TV) April 14, 1953; 30 minutes; black and white

**Cast**
Martin Kingsley, Irene Vernon, JAMES DEAN

Murder mysteries and psychological thrillers were the forte` of this anthology series, hosted by  Richard Stark. Several episodes were directed by Yul Brynner, Sidney Lumet and John Frankenheimer. James Dean appeared on *Danger* four times, first as a safecracker in an episode entitled "No Room."

**T13  Treasury Men in Action** (NBC-TV) April 16, 1953; 30 minutes; black and white

Dean returned to *Treasury Men in Action* for "The Case of the Sawed-Off Shotgun."

**T14  Tales of Tomorrow** (ABC-TV) May 1, 1953; 30 minutes; black and white

**Credits**
Directed by Don Medford; Written by Manya Starr; Produced by Mort Abrahams

**Cast**
Rod Steiger, Margaret Phillips, JAMES DEAN

*Tales of Tomorrow*, the first science-fiction series aimed at adults, combined original stories with adaptations of novels by Jules Verne and H.G. Wells. In "The Evil Within," Rod Steiger plays a scientist who invents an evil-inducing serum, that is accidently consumed by his wife (Margaret Phillips). Dean plays a bit part as Steiger's lab assistant.

**T15  Campbell Soundstage** (NBC-TV) July 17, 1953; 30 minutes; black and white

**Credits**
Directed by  Don Medford; Written by S. Lee Pogostin; Produced by Martin Horrell

### Cast
JAMES DEAN (JOE ADAMS), Susan Douglas

In "Something For an Empty Briefcase," Dean starred as a troubled youth, bordering on juvenile delinquency but trying to go straight. He commits one last crime to raise money for the purchase of a briefcase, which he hopes will represent the first step toward a more respectable life.

## T16  Studio One Summer Theatre (CBS-TV) August 17, 1953; 60 minutes; black and white

### Credits
Directed by Paul Nickell; Written by Adrian Spies and Thomas Walsh

### Cast
Gene Lyons, Ralph Dunn, JAMES DEAN, Betsy Palmer

Dean's co-starring role in "Sentence of Death" marked his last appearance on the longest-running and arguably the most revered of television's early anthology series.

## T17  Danger (CBS-TV) August 25, 1953; 30 minutes; black and white

### Credits
Directed by John Peyser; Written by Frank Gregory; Produced by Franklin Heller

### Cast
Walter Hampden, JAMES DEAN, Betsy Palmer

Dean appeared in an episode entitled "Death is My Neighbor." Producer Franklin Heller threatened to fire Dean at one point, over his frequent criticism of the script, but director Walter Hampden convinced Heller to change his mind. "I think he's going to be a big star," he said. (see B   )

## T18  The Big Story (NBC-TV) September 11, 1953; 30 minutes; black and white

### Credits

Directed by Stuart Rosenberg; Narrated by Bob Sloane

### Cast
JAMES DEAN, John Kerr, Wendy Drew, Carl Frank, Donald McKee, Ken Walken, Bobby Nick, Susan Harris

On *The Big Story*, reporters from newspapers across the country would appear in dramatizations of their most significant news stories. Popular subjects included the uncoverage of corruption, crime solving, national scandals and emotional human interest pieces. The episode in which Dean appeared was inspired by a story that appeared in the Joplin, Missouri *Globe and News Herald*, written by Rex Newman.

## T19 Omnibus (CBS-TV) October 4, 1953; 90 minutes; black and white

### Credits
Directed by Andrew McCullough; Written by William Inge; Produced by Fred Rickey

### Cast
Jessica Tandy, Hume Cronyn, Ed Binns, Frank McHugh, JAMES DEAN

Alastair Cooke was the host of this prestigious cultural series. Opera, symphony, ballet, dramatic plays and true-life adventure films were presented on this rarest of broadcasts that ran without commercials (*Omnibus* was financed by the Ford Foundation TV-Radio Workshop). Playwright William Inge (*Splendor in the Grass*) debuted his play "Glory in Flower" on the premiere episode of the second season, and suggested James Dean for the role of a troubled adolescent.

## T20 Kraft Television Theatre (NBC-TV) October 14, 1953; 60 minutes; black and white

### Credits
Directed and produced by Maury Holland; Written by George Roy Hill

### Cast
Michael Higgins, Joan Potter, David White, George Roy Hill, JAMES DEAN, Rusty Lane, Larry Fletcher, Addison Richards

A student cheating scandal that threatens to destroy a college honor society is the subject of an episode entitled "Keep Our Honor Bright." Dean, in what had already become a pattern, plays a distraught young man whose problems compel him to attempt suicide. Writer George Roy Hill won an Academy Award in 1973 for his direction of *The Sting*.

**T21**  **Campbell Soundstage** (NBC-TV) October 16, 1953; 30 minutes; black and white

> **Cast**
> JAMES DEAN (HANK BRADON), Georgann Johnson

In "Life Sentence," Dean plays an ex-convict.

**T22**  **Kraft Television Theatre** (NBC-TV) November 11, 1953; 60 minutes; black and white

> **Credits**
> Directed and produced by Dick Dunlap; Written by Rod Serling

> **Cast**
> JAMES DEAN (JOE HARRIS), Naomi Riordan, Robert Simon, Ted Osborn, Rudolph Weiss

The great Rod Serling penned "A Long Time Till Dawn," a character study of a convicted felon named Joe Harris who is both poet and gangster, "violence with blue eyes." After his release from prison, Joe tries unsuccessfully to go straight. Fans rank "A Long Time Till Dawn" among Dean's most accomplished performances in any medium.

**T23**  **Armstrong Circle Theatre** (NBC-TV)  November 17, 1953; 30 minutes; black and white

> **Credits**
> Directed by James Sheldon; Written by George Lowther; Produced by Hudson Faussett

> **Cast**
> Gene Lockhart, JAMES DEAN (JOEY FRAZIER), Vaughn Taylor, Donalee Marans, John Dennis

Dramas that were suitable for viewing by the whole family were the specialty of *Armstrong Circle Theatre*. In "The Bells of Cockaigne," Dean plays a blue-collar laborer who has trouble supporting his wife and child. Fans remember this show primarily because Dean appears shirtless.

## T24 Robert Montgomery Presents the Johnson's Wax Program (CBS-TV), March 30, 1954; 60 minutes; black and white

### Credits
Directed by James Sheldon; Written by Sandra Michael; Produced and hosted by Robert Montgomery

### Cast
Ed Begley, Dorothy Gish, Vaughn Taylor, JAMES DEAN (PAUL ZALENKA), Reba Tassell, John Connell, John Dennis, Joseph Foley, Nancy Sheridan

Of all the numerous dramatic series of television's golden age, *Robert Montgomery Presents...* can boast one of the most distinguished rosters of guest stars, among them Helen Hayes, James Cagney and Claudette Colbert. "Harvest," the Thanksgiving, 1953 episode, featured Dean as a farm boy who joins the navy after being jilted by his girlfriend.

## T25 Danger (CBS-TV) March 30, 1954; 30 minutes; black and white

### Credits
Directed and produced by Andrew McCullough

### Cast
Lydia Reed, Lee Bergere, JAMES DEAN (AUGIE)

"The Little Woman" episode of *Danger* contains Dean's most significant work on that series; he plays another juvenile delinquent, who is running from the law and takes shelter in a little girl's playhouse.

## T26 Philco TV Playhouse (NBC-TV) September 5, 1954; 60 minutes; black and white

### Credits
Directed by Jeffrey Hayden; Written by Sam Hall; Produced by Gordon Duff

### Cast
Kurt Kasznar, Gusti Huber, JAMES DEAN (ROB), Barbara O'Neil

*Philco TV Playhouse* is best remembered for its television adaptations of Broadway dramas and musicals, in which original cast members reprised their roles. "Run Like a Thief" was broadcast later in the series' run, when this popular practice had been discontinued. A waiter finds a valuable bracelet that belongs to his boss, and after much soul-searching he decides to give it to his wife. Dean plays another waiter, whose admiration for his colleague is destroyed.

**T27   Danger** (CBS-TV) November 9, 1954; 30 minutes; black and white

### Credits
Directed by John Frankenheimer

### Cast
Mildred Dunnock, JAMES DEAN

Dean's last appearance on *Danger* came in an episode entitled "Padlocks." Director Frankenheimer's subsequent credits include *The Manchurian Candidate* (1962) and *Birdman of Alcatraz* (1962).

**T28   General Electric Theatre** (CBS-TV) November 14, 1954; 30 minutes; black and white

### Credits
Directed by Don Medford; Written by Arnold Schulman, based on a story by Sherwood Anderson; Produced by Mort Abrahams

### Cast
JAMES DEAN, Natalie Wood, Eddie Albert, Roy Glenn, Eve March, Leon Taylor, Gloria Costillo, Fiona Hale

Ronald Reagan was the host of this anthology series that ranked a bit lower on the quality depth chart than *Studio One* or *Kraft Television Theatre*. James Dean's first appearance, however, is memorable above and beyond his participation because of his performance opposite Natalie Wood, with whom he would co-star in *Rebel Without a Cause* (see F5). The episode, entitled "I'm A Fool," casts Dean as a lovestruck farm boy who tries to impress a classy, beautiful girl (Wood) by creating a false identity. Dean filmed the episode after completing work on *East of Eden*, and it represents one of his few television credits to be shot in Hollywood, instead of New York.

## T29 General Electric Theatre (CBS-TV) December 12,1954; 30 minutes; black and white

### Credits
Directed by Don Medford; Written by Arthur Steuer

### Cast
Ronald Reagan, JAMES DEAN, Constance Ford, Jack Simmons

Reagan stepped out of his role as host of *General Electric Theatre* to star in"The Dark, Dark Hour" as a small-town doctor whose home is invaded by a gun-toting delinquent (guess who). The doctor and his wife (Constance Ford) are held prisoner by the borderline psychotic felon and his partner (Jack Simmons), who was wounded in a robbery and must now seek treatment from his captive. The casting alone makes this one of the more fascinating artifacts in the Dean canon.

## T30 The U.S. Steel Hour (ABC-TV) January 4, 1955; 60 minutes; black and white

### Credits
Directed by Vincent J. Donehue; Written by Arthur Arent, from a play by Henri Bernstein

### Cast
Paul Lukas, JAMES DEAN, Mary Astor, Diana Lynn, Patric Knowles

In "The Thief," Dean plays the youngest son of a wealthy family who is suspected of stealing money.

## T31 Lux Video Theatre (NBC-TV) March 10, 1955; 30 minutes; black and white

Dean does not appear in the March 10, 1955 presentation of "The Life of Emile Zola," however he does appear in a live interview conducted just prior to its broadcast. He talked about his work on *East of Eden* (see F4).

## T32 Schlitz Playhouse of Stars (CBS-TV) May 6, 1955; 60 minutes; black and white

### Credits
Directed by Justus Addiss; Written by Walter C. Brown;
Produced by William Self

### Cast
JAMES DEAN (JEFF LATHAM), Murvyn Vye, Pat Hardy, Edgar
Stehli, Charles Wagenheim, Voltaire Perkins, Robert Williams

In his final dramatic role on television, James Dean stars in "The Unlighted Road" as a teenage drifter who tries to start his life over after getting a job in a coffee shop. Unfortunately, his plans go awry when he unwittingly becomes involved with a criminal gang. The show was rerun, a first for the *Schlitz Playhouse of Stars*, after Dean's death five months later.

## T33   Commercial (all networks-TV) 1955; black and white

On September 17, 1955, James Dean and actor Gig Young taped a public service television commercial for the National Safety Council. Young asks Dean for his opinion about fast driving on the highway. "I used to fly around, but, you know, I took a lot of unnecessary chances on the highway," Dean replied. "Then I started racing, and now when I drive on the highways I'm extra cautious." Young then asks, "Do you have any special advice for the young people who drive?" "Take it easy driving," says Dean, "the life you save might be mine." Less then two weeks later, Dean was killed in a car accident on a California highway.

## T34   The Colgate Variety  Hour (NBC-TV) November 27, 1955; 60 minutes; black and white

*Modern Screen* magazine presents a posthumous award to James Dean.

## T35   The Ed Sullivan Show (CBS-TV) October 14, 1956; 60 minutes; black and white

Just four days after the premiere of *Giant* (1956), *The Ed Sullivan Show* aired a special salute to James Dean. Sullivan was accused of stealing the idea for the segment from Steve Allen, who had also planned a Dean tribute.

## T36   The Steve Allen Show (NBC-TV) October 14, 1956; 60 minutes; black and white

Allen's tribute to James Dean, originally scheduled for broadcast on

October 21, 1956, was moved up one week to compete opposite a similar piece on *The Ed Sulllivan Show* (see T35).

## T37  Wide World of Entertainment  (ABC-TV) November 13, 1974; 90 minutes; color and black and white

Peter Lawford interviews Sal Mineo, Sammy Davis, Jr., Steve Allen, Natalie Wood and Leonard Rosenman about their favorite memories of James Dean, in this documentary entitled "Memories of a Gentle Rebel." The program was directed by Jack Haley, Jr., written by Al Ramrus, and produced by Al Ramrus and Ronald Lyon.

## T38  James Dean (NBC-TV) February 19, 1976; 100 minutes; color

### Credits
Directed by Robert Butler; Written by Bill Bast, based on his book; Produced by Bill Bast and John Forbes

### Cast
Stephen McHattie (James Dean), Michael Brandon (Bill Bast), Candy Clark, Amy Irving, Meg Foster, Brooke Adams, Katherine Helmond

A made-for-TV movie biography of James Dean, based on one of the best and most accurate books about his life, *James Dean* by Bill Bast (see B009). Bill Bast was a close friend of Dean's since they were both students at UCLA,

## T39  Hollywood Close-Up September 30, 1983; 30 minutes; color and black and white

This entertainment news series, similar in style to *Entertainment Tonight*, devoted an entire program to James Dean, on the twenty-eighth anniversary of his death. Bill Bast, Ursula Andress, Martin Landau and James Whitmore shared remembrances. The segment was directed by Craig Haffner, produced by Arthur Drooker and narrated by Ernie Anderson.

## T40  Entertainment Tonight (syndicated-TV) September, 1985; 30 minutes; color

On the thirtieth anniversary of James Dean's death, *Entertainment*

*Tonight* presented "The Legend That Won't Die," Host Mary Hart introduced film footage of Dean and interviews with Marcus and Ortense Winslow (relatives), Bill Bast, Jim Backus, Dennis Hopper, Burl Ives, Elizabeth Taylor, Adeline Nall (teacher), Carroll Baker, Corey Allen, Martin Landau, and Ernie Tripke, the California Highway Patrol officer who was at the scene of the crash that killed James Dean.

**T41   Show Biz Today** (CNN-Cable) September 30, 1985; 30 minutes; color

Another thirtieth anniversary tribute, combining film footage with numerous interviews. Eartha Kitt, Jim Backus, Corey Allen, Ernie Tripke and Martin Landau are among those who share remembrances. Sandy Kenyon hosts.

**T42   Forever James Dean** (Cinemax-Cable) 1988; 60 minutes; color and black and white

A documentary on Dean written, produced and directed by Ara Chekmayan, and narrated by Bob Gunton. Jeff Lawenda and Michael Yudin served as executive producers, and David Dalton, author of two books on Dean, was a consultant. Other research was conducted by David Loehr and Susan Bluttman. Those interviewed include actors Corey Allen, Jack Grinnage, Julie Harris, Beverly Long, Frank Mazzola, and Steffi Sidney, friends George Barris, Bill Bast, Rex Bright, Bob Pulley, and Bob Roth , teacher Adeline Nall, artist Kenneth Kendall, and photographer Frank Worth.

**T43   A Current Affair** (Fox-TV) May 10, 1989; 30 minutes; color

A hyperbolic story, introduced by Maury Povich, about a "jinx" that has followed James Dean's Porsche ever since Dean was killed while driving it. Four of Dean's friends, George Barris, Lew Bracker, Maila Nurmi and Leonard Rosenman, were interviewed.

**T44   A Current Affair** (Fox-TV) September 27, 1989; 30 minutes; color

Several clips from Dean's rarely-seen appearances on live television dramas are presented.

# 6

# DISCOGRAPHY

**D 1    JAMES  DEAN**
(1955, Warner Bros BS-2843-LP). Later titled *The James Dean Story*.

A compilation of music and dialog exerpts from *East of Eden* (featuring Dean, Jo Van Fleet, Raymond Massey, Julie Harris and Barbara Baxley), *Rebel Without a Cause* (with Dean, Jim Backus and Ann Doran), and *Giant* (with Dean, Rock Hudson, Elizabeth Taylor, Mercedes McCambridge, Charles Watts, Monte Hale, Chill Wills and Carroll Baker).

**D 2    JAMES  DEAN  ON  THE  AIR**
(Sandy Hook Records 2103-LP)

Broadcasts of two of James Dean's television dramas, *The Unlighted Road* and *I'm a Fool*.

**D 3    JAMES  DEAN  ON  CONGA  DRUMS  IN  AN  AD-LIB  JAM  SESSION**
(Romeo Records-LP)

An amateur, audiotape recording of James Dean on conga drums and Bob Romeo on flute, performing two of Dean's compositions, *Dean's Lament* and *Jungle Rhythms*. The songs were later released by Romeo on a 45 r.p.m. record.

**D 4    FIFTY  YEARS  OF  FILM**
(1973, Warner Bros. 3XX2737-LP)

Three discs of dialog excerpts from Warner Bros. motion picture soundtracks, from 1923 to 1973. James Dean is heard with Raymond Massey and Richard Davalos from *East of Eden*, with Jim Backus and Ann Doran from *Rebel Without a Cause*, and with Rock Hudson, Elizabeth Taylor and Chill Wills from *Giant*.

# 7

# BIBLIOGRAPHY

## Books

**B001**  Adams, Cindy. *Lee Strasberg: The Imperfect Genius of the Actors Studio.* Doubleday, New York, 1980

A biography of Lee Strasberg, an Austrian immigrant who became the artistic director of The Actors Studio in 1948, and one of the most influential acting coaches of the New York stage. According to author Cindy Adams, Strasberg was drawn to "highly gifted freaks," and loved the "negative-positive level of genius in the crazily desperately talented Kim Stanley and Geraldine Page and Jimmy Dean."

**B002**  Adams, Leith and Keith Burns. *James Dean: Behind the Scenes.* Birch Lane Press, New York, 1990.

Clearly the best of the book-length photo journals of Dean's life available. Many never-before published photos from the Warner Bros. archives, including a wonderful photo of Dean and Marlon Brando, are mixed with photos taken by Dean on the sets of his three Warners films. The book also reprints studio memos, telegrams and letters from coworkers who figured prominently in Dean's career, including Jack Warner, Elia Kazan and Nicholas Ray.

**B003**  Alexander, Paul. *Boulevard of Broken Dreams: The Life, Times and Legend of James Dean.* Viking, New York, 1994.

Insightful in its examination of the James Dean cult following ("Deaners"), but Alexander's steamy biography is more preoccupied with its subject's sex life than with his motion picture legacy.

**B004**  Anger, Kenneth. *Hollywood Babylon II*. E.P. Dutton, New York, 1984.

A follow-up to *Hollywood Babylon*, Kenneth Anger's sordid collection of gruesome photos and venemous stories about the dark side of fame. James Dean, the author contends, was a sadomasochist who frequented gay bars, and was sexually aroused by cigarette burns.

**B005**  Arens, Axel. *James Dean Photographs*. W.W. Norton Books, New York, 1992

**B006**  Astor, Mary. *My Story: An Autobiography*. Doubleday, New York, 1959.

Mary Astor, whose impressive motion picture career spans five decades and includes such classics as *The Maltese Falcon* and *The Palm Beach Story*, appeared opposite James Dean in a 1955 episode of *The U.S. Steel Hour* entitled *The Thief* (see T30). She admits in her autobiography that Dean, "in his quiet, thoughtful, mumbling way," stole the production.

**B007**  Backus, Jim. *Rocks on the Roof*. G.P. Putnam's Sons, New York, 1958.

Jim Backus played James Dean's weak-willed father in *Rebel Without a Cause*. One chapter of his book is devoted to Dean, whom Backus describes as "strong as a bull," and "frightening" in his intensity, but he also admits, "I liked him." Backus relates how Dean asked him to do the voice of Mr. Magoo, which Dean then picked up and learned to mimic so well that it was incorporated into the film.

**B008**  Baker, Carroll. *Baby Doll*. Arbor House, New York, 1983.

Baker devotes almost twenty pages to several anecdotes from the sets of *Rebel Without a Cause* and *Giant*. Dean's elusive, true personality comes through more clearly in Baker's recollections of the actor's teasing of Natalie Wood and his late-night motorcycle rides than it does in several Dean biographies. First-rate.

**B009**  Bast, William. *James Dean*. Ballantine, New York, 1956.

The first significant biography of James Dean, and though long out of print it is still regarded by fans as one of the best. Bast, who met and befriended Dean in 1950, when both men were studying acting at UCLA, was a  close confidante until Dean's death. In 1976, Bast adapted his book into the television movie *James Dean* (see T-T2).

**B010** Beath, Warren Newton. *The Death of James Dean*. Grove Press, New York, 1986.

For the devoted more than the casual fan, Beath reconstructs in painstaking detail the last days of James Dean, and the inquest that followed his death, ultimately concluding that it was Donald Turnupseed, and not Dean, who was responsible for the tragic auto accident. The balance of the book is comprised of a personal and candid account of the author's own Dean obsession, his associations with other disciples, and his regarding of any slight scrap of memoribilia as a treasured artifact. Sincere, but very sad.

**B011** Boller, Paul F. and Ronald L. Davis. *Hollywood Anecdotes*. William Morrow & Co., New York, 1987.

Ann Doran, who played Dean's mother in *Rebel Without a Cause*, recalls a harrowing motorcycle ride she took with her "son," during a break in filming.She also found Dean becoming attached to her, as his search continued for the mother he barely knew.

**B012** Bosworth, Patricia. *Montgomery Clift*. Harcourt Brace Jovanovich, New York, 1978.

Bosworth contends that Clift was James Dean's idol, though Clift thought Dean was "weird" after seeing him in a television drama.

**B013** Brando, Marlon. *Songs My Mother Taught Me*. Random House, New York, 1994.

"Like me, (Dean) became a symbol of social change during the 1950s by happenstance," writes Brando, reflecting on his first meeting with Dean on the set of *East of Eden*. "He made it clear that he was not only mimicking my acting but also what he believed was my lifestyle." Brando offers several interesting insights into Dean's character in this enjoyable biography.

**B014** Brean, Joel. *Rebels United: The Enduring Reality of James Dean*. Brean-Jones Publishing, 1984.

A self-published account of the author's supposed encounters with James Dean after the actor's death. From 1976 to 1982, Brean contends that Dean's ghost appeared to him, and offered opinions on the nuclear arms race and eastern philosophy.

**B015**  Carey, Gary. *Marlon Brando: The Only Contender*. St. Martin's
Press, New York, 1985.

Carey leaves no doubt about his own views on the "Brando vs. Dean"
debate; "He was the most flagrant and successful of the Brando
imitators," writes Carey of Dean. "A surprising number of people who
otherwise have good taste prefer Dean to Brando."

**B016**  Collins, Joan. *Past Imperfect*. Simon & Schuster, New York,
1984.

The star of *Dynasty* and the best *Star Trek* episode ever recounts her
one meeting with James Dean, at a dinner party during the filming of
*Giant*. "I was particularly mesmerized by his eyes, which were a deep,
piercing blue and could change instantly from a look of sullen brooding to
an expression of extreme mischievousness."

**B017**  Corley, Ed. *Farewell My Slightly Tarnished Hero*. Dodd, Mead
and Co., New York, 1971.

A fictional biography of James Dean, that is now something of a
collector's item.

**B018**  Cronyn, Hume. *A Terrible Liar*. William Morrow & Co., New York,
1991.

In 1953, Hume Cronyn starred with his wife, Jessica Tandy, and with
James Dean in the William Inge television play *Glory in Flower*, which was
presented on the *Omnibus* series. He describes Dean as "not rude, not
quite arrogant but with a manner that said 'I'm here--pay attention--and I
don't give a damn what you think.'" Cronyn recalls being outraged at
Dean's sudden improvisation during rehersal, but was impressed with his
performance.

**B019**  Cunningham, Terry. *James Dean: The Way it Was*. Electric
Reader, London, 1983.

A trade paperback biography, published only in Great Britain.

**B020**  Dalton, David. *James Dean: The Mutant King*. Straight Arrow
Books, Coronado, California, 1974.

Despite its odd title, one of the least "tabloid" of the Dean biographies. Dalton examines in scholarly detail the forces that shaped Dean as a performer and a human being.

**B021** Dalton, David. *James Dean: American Icon.* St. Martin's Press, New York, 1984.

Dalton's second book on James Dean is first-rate, from its Andy Warhol cover to its excellent selection of photographs. A classy coffee-table book with a perfect balance of art and text, *James Dean: American Icon* may be a bit esoteric for the casual fan, and is occasionally guilty of over-reaching in its assessment of the Dean legacy, but it is arguably the best one-stop shopping volume available.

**B022** Davis, Jr., Sammy. *Hollywood in a Suitcase.* William Morrow & Co., New York, 1980.

Actor-singer-dancer Sammy Davis, Jr. takes the entertainment community to task for not recognizing sooner the brilliance of James Dean as an actor, and his discomfort as a human being; "Hollywood hardly touched him as a person. It is to our eternal shame as a community that we passed him off as a bit of a slob. He *was* difficult to talk to, but we should have tried harder."

**B023** Dawber, Martin. *Wish You Were Here, Jimmy Dean.* Columbus Books, London, 1989.

Published only in Great Britain, this frequently inaccurate biography is distinguished only by its Kenneth Kendall illustrations.

**B024** Devillers, Marceau. *James Dean on Location.* Sidgwick & Jackson, Great Britain, 1987.

A biography originally written in French, and later translated for publication in Great Britain.

**B025** Eisenschitz, Bernard. *Nicholas Ray.* Faber & Faber, London, 1993.

This exhaustively-reserached biography of director Nicholas Ray may provide the most insight into Ray's friendship and working relationship with Dean on *Rebel Without a Cause.*

**B026** Ellis, Royston. *The Rebel.* Consul Books, Great Britain, 1962.

An early biography of Dean, second only to William Bast's *James Dean*. The book has been out of print for over a decade.

**B027** Elman, Di. *James Dean: Just Once More*. Dayenu Productions, Santa Barbara, California, 1993.

A self-published collection of Dean-related poetry and photos.

**B028** Ferber, Edna. *A Kind of Magic*. Doubleday, Garden City, NJ, 1963.

Edna Ferber was the author of *Giant*. "Occasionally--rarely--one encounters a dazzling human being who is obviously marked for destruction," she writes. "Such a one was this young Jimmy Dean. Only two or three times have I encountered an example of the brilliant and ill-fated." As the character Jett Rink, she thought him "miscast, but enthralling."

**B029** Fuchs, Wolfgang. *James Dean: Footsteps of a Giant*. Taco, West Germany, 1986.

A German trade paperback biography with a generous selection of photographs.

**B030** Garfield, David. *A Player's Place*. MacMillan, New York, 1980.

Garfield's fascinating history of The Actor's Studio devotes several pages to Dean's time with the Studio. "It is one of the larger ironies of the history of The Actor's Studio," Garfield observes, "that James Dean, the young actor whose name comes so readily to mind whenever the studio is mentioned. . .was very inhibited there and worked very little in class. It is a rare Studio member who can recollect a scene in which James Dean appeared."

**B031** Gilmore, John. *The Real James Dean*. Pyramid Books, New York, 1975.

An actor and poet who first met James Dean in 1952, John Gilmore suggests in his book that he and Dean were lovers, but offers little else of note.

**B032** Griffin, Merv. *Merv*. Simon & Schuster, New York, 1980.

Talk show host Merv Griffin recalls an incident on the set of *East of Eden*, when James Dean met Humphrey Bogart. After trying unsuccessfully to maintain a conversation, Bogie grabbed the sullen Dean by the lapels and yelled, "You little punk! When I talk to you, you look in my eyes, you understand? Who the hell do you think you are, you two-bit nothing?"

**B033** Grobel, Lawrence. *Conversations With Capote.* New American Library, New York, 1985.

Author Truman Capote speaks derisively of Dean, whom he had known during the actor's years in New York. "I never thought anything about him as an actor. I didn't think he had any quality at all."

**B034** Guinness, Alec. *Blessings in Disguise.* Alfred A. Knopf, New York, 1986.

Distinguished British actor Alec Guinness met James Dean on September 23, 1955, at Villa Capri, a Los Angeles restaurant. Dean was showing off his new Porsche. "If you get in that car you will be found dead in it by this time next week," Guinness told Dean, who laughed at the warning. They had dinner together that night. One week later, Dean was dead.

**B035** Halliwell, Leslie. *The Filmgoer's Companion.* Hill and Wang, New York, 1977.

The sixth edition of this venerable research publication lists James Dean as a "moody young American actor", whose death "caused an astonishing world-wide outburst of emotional necrophilia."

**B036** Herndon, Venable. *James Dean: A Short Life.* Doubleday, New York, 1974.

The slew of James Dean biographies published in the early 1970s probably prevented this interesting, well-written book from receiving the attention it deserved. A good, straightforward, factual treatment.

**B037** Higham, Charles. *Brando: The Unauthorized Biography.* New American Library, New York, 1987.

According to Charles Higham, Dean "fell futilely in love with Marlon Brando after viewing *The Wild One,* and beseiged him with phone calls."

**B038** Hirschhorn, Clive. *The Warner Bros. Story.* Crown Publishers, New York, 1979.

Capsule reviews of *East of Eden*, *Rebel Without a Cause* and *Giant*, each accompanied by one photo.

**B 0 3 9** Hopper, Hedda. *The Whole Truth and Nothing But.* Doubleday, New York, 1963.

Legendary gossip columnist Hedda Hopper first wrote negatively of James Dean ("They've brought out from New York another dirty-shirt-tail actor"), but was impressed enough by his performance in *East of Eden* to request an interview. After being charmed by Dean, she became an enthusiastic supporter.

**B 0 4 0** Hoskyns, Barney and David Loehr. *James Dean: Shooting Star.* Doubleday, New York, 1990.

Photographs from the collection of James Dean Gallery curator David Loehr are accompanied by Barney Hoskyns' uninspired text.

**B 0 4 1** Houseman, John. *Front and Center.* Simon & Schuster, New York, 1979.

Actor-director John Houseman thought Dean was "the most exciting young actor since Marlon Brando," after seeing *East of Eden*. He befriended the actor, and wanted Dean to play the lead in *The Cobweb* (see W5) but studio intervention prevented the deal from being made.

**B 0 4 2** Howlett, John. *James Dean: A Biography.* Plexus Publishing, Great Britain, 1975.

Original interviews with Elia Kazan, Nicholas Ray and Natalie Wood are the highlights of this standard but proficient biography.

**B 0 4 3** Hudson, Rock and Sara Davidson. *Rock Hudson: His Story.* William Morrow & Co., New York, 1986.

The antagonism between Rock Hudson and James Dean was no secret. "I didn't particularly like him, personally. But that didn't matter," writes Hudson. "Jimmy was certainly effective in the role, especially in the younger part."

**B 0 4 4** Hyams, Joe. *Mislaid in Hollywood.* Peter H. Wyden, New York, 1973.

Veteran Hollywood writer Joe Hyams devotes a chapter in his book of show business stories to his friendship with Dean, and his astonishment after seeing *East of Eden* for the first time; "When the film ended I was both drained and exhilarated. There was no doubt in my mind then that James Dean was going to be Hollywood's next big star."

**B045** Hyams, Joe. *James Dean: Little Boy Lost.* Warner Books, New York, 1994.

Joe Hyams' graphic descriptions of Dean's sexual escapades with a variety of partners, male and female, grabbed the headlines in reviews, but this is actually one of the more balanced and clear-eyed biographies available. Hyams knew Dean and his inner circle, and coaxed many former friends to speak on the record for the first time. Their comments unintentionally reveal how Dean's associates humored his eccentricities, often with selfish motivations. The riveting final chapter, which recounts how several of Dean's friends, family members and costars heard the news of his death, is superbly constructed.

**B046** Kazan, Elia. *Kazan: A Life.* Alfred A. Knopf, New York, 1988.

Extensive coverage of the making of *East of Eden*, and how director Elia Kazan manipulated James Dean in various scenes to coax the amazing performance that launched Dean's career.

**B047** Kelley, Kitty. *Elizabeth Taylor: The Last Star.* G.K. Hall, Boston, 1982.

Though one cannot always take Kelley's prose at face value, she paints a captivating portrait of the friendship between Elizabeth Taylor and James Dean, which began on the set of *Giant*.

**B048** Kitt, Eartha. *Alone With Me.* Regency, Chicago, 1976.

Actress and nightclub entertainer Eartha Kitt was one of Dean's closest confidantes. "Jamie and I were like brother and sister," she writes of their friendship. "He told me in fact he thought of me as a sister. Our relationship was strictly platonic and spiritual."

**B049** Kreidl, John. *Nicholas Ray.* Twayne, Boston, 1977.

This authorized biography of *Rebel Without a Cause* director Nicholas Ray contains many fascinating quotes about Ray's working relationship and friendship with Dean.

**B050** Levant, Oscar. *The Unimportance of Being Oscar*. G.P. Putman's Sons, New York, 1968.

The eccentric, sharp-witted actor/musician Oscar Levant relates a delightful anecdote that illustrates the kinder, gentler side of the brooding rebel. After learning that Levant's young daughter was a fan, Dean dropped in for a surprise visit, and thanked the starstruck girl for her devotion.

**B051** Martinetti, Ronald. *The James Dean Story*. Pinnacle Books, New York, 1975.

A well-reviewed biography that received limited distribution, and that can only be found in collector's bookstores.

**B052** Massey , Raymond. *A Hundred Different Lives*. Little, Brown & Co., Boston, 1979.

Raymond Massey did not enjoy the experience of working with James Dean on *East of Eden*. "He approached everything with a chip on his shoulder," writes Massey. "Jimmy never knew his lines before he walked on the set, rarely had command of them when the camera rolled and even if he had was often inaudible. Simple technicalities, such as moving on cue and finding his marks, were beneath his consdieration."

**B053** McCann, Graham. *Rebel Males: Clift, Brando and Dean*. Rutgers University Press, New Brunswick, NJ, 1991.

Author McCann devotes forty pages to James Dean's life and career, with quotes from Elia Kazan, Dennis Hopper and Francois Truffaut.

**B054** Morella, Joe and Edward Epstein. *Rebels: The Rebel Hero in Films*. Citadel Press, New York, 1971.

The authors devote one chapter to James Dean in this compilation of movie rebels. The biography consists of recycled information.

**B055** Morrissey, Stephen. *James Dean is Not Dead*. Babylon Books, Great Britain, 1983.

Stephen Morrissey is best known as the lead vocalist for the British art rock group The Smiths. More a tribute to its subject than a biography, *James Dean is Not Dead* adds little of interest to the Dean canon.

**B056** Oumano, Elena. *Paul Newman.* St. Martin's Press, New York, 1987.

Paul Newman was often compared to James Dean in his early career, and was not flattered or pleased by the comparisons. He thought Dean had "a lot like a little boy point of view."

**B057** Parish, James Robert. *Actors Television Credits.* Scarecrow Press, Tononto, 1973.

A list of most of James Dean's television appearances.

**B058** Parish, James Robert. *Gays and Lesbians in Mainstream Cinema.*

**B059** Riese, Randall. *The Unabridged James Dean.* Contemporary Books, Chicago, 1991.

Organized like an encyclopedia, this massive, 600-page book explores Dean's life, work and legacy in astonishing detail. Fans who need to know the name of the ambulance driver who arrived on the scene of Dean's fatal crash, the addresses of every home in which Dean lived, or his social security number will find the minutiae they crave in this comprehensive volume.

**B060** Ross, Walter S. *The Immortal.* Simon & Schuster, New York, 1958.

A fictional biography of James Dean, who is called Johnny Preston. Movie rights to the book were purchased by MGM, and George Hamilton was signed to star as Preston, but the film was never produced.

**B061** Roth, Beulah and Sanford. *James Dean.* Pomegranate Books, New York, 1983.

Sanford Roth's photographs of Dean are the subject of this book. His wife Beulah provides the captions, which appear in English, French and Japanese.

**B062** Schary, Dore. *Heyday.* Little, Brown & Co., Boston, 1979.

Dore Schary was the vice president in charge of production at MGM between 1948 and 1956. He met with Dean in 1955, to discuss the possibilty of the actor playing boxer Rocky Graziano in *Somebody Up There Likes Me.* Schary tried to put Dean at ease by poking fun at his studio mogul image; "Should I be in the back of the desk with a fat cigar? Or should I swing a golf club or polo mallet?" Dean smiled at the joke, and the meeting continued.

**B063**  Schatt, Roy. *James Dean: A Portrait*. Delilah Books, New York, 1982.

Photographer Roy Schatt shares his recollections of the lessons he gave Dean in taking pictures, and the photos he took of Dean from February, 1954 to December, 1954, including the famous "torn sweater" series. The book also contains photos taken by Dean of Roy Schatt and other friends, including Martin Landau.

**B064**  St. Michael, Mick. *James Dean: In His Own Words*. Omnibus Press, Great Britain, 1989.

A compilation of Dean quotes, arranged chronologically, that have appeared in almost every biography of Dean. The introductory text is basic and banal ("Journalists and columnists now gathered around the Warner Bros. lot like bees around a honey pot, and Jimmy was the Queen Bee"), but to the author's credit they include quotations that are less than flattering. At a mere 64 pages, however, *James Dean: In His Own Words* contains little that can't be found elsewhere.

**B065**  Stock, Dennis. *James Dean Revisited*. Viking, New York, 1978.

Another book of photos, that is interesting mainly for the series of photographs of James Dean's family in Fairmount, Indiana.

**B066**  Taylor, Elizabeth. *An Informal Memoir*. Harper & Row, New York, 1965.

Elizabeth Taylor recalls the special friendship she shared with James Dean on the set of *Giant*, and the terrible day when she heard of Dean's death.

**B067**  Thomas, T.T. *James Dean*. Popular Library, 1957.

The first fictional biography of James Dean.

**B068**  Thomson, David. *A Biographical Dictionary of Film*. William Morrow and Co., New York, 1981.

A brief, biographical sketch of James Dean.

**B069** Tysl, Robert Wayne. *Continuity and Evolution in a Public Symbol: An Investigation Into the Creation and Communication of the James Dean Image in Mid-Century America.* Michigan State University Press, Michigan, 1965.

A 670-page thesis, examining the emergence and growth of the James Dean legend.

**B070** Volpe, Dante. *The Last James Dean Book.* William Morrow and Co., New York, 1974.

Illustrations of James Dean created by Dante Volpe, including line drawings of a nude Dean. The title is both misleading and inaccurate.

**B071** Whitman, Mark. *The Films of James Dean.* Greenhaven Press, New York, 1974.

Since James Dean starred in only three films, it's hard to justify a book devoted to coverage of his "filmography." The basic text is accompanied by a generous selection of photos.

**B072** Winters, Shelley. *Shelley II: The Middle of My Century.* Simon & Schuster, New York, 1989.

Shelley Winters recalls an evening of dinner at Hollywood's Hamburger Hamlet and seeing the film *On the Waterfront*, accompanied by James Dean, Nicholas Ray and Marilyn Monroe.

### Magazines

**B073** Adams, Nick. "The James Dean I Knew." *Screen Stars*, September 1956.

**B074** Adams, Nick. "Jimmy's Happiest Moments." *Modern Screen*, October 1956.

**B075** Adams, Nick. "Jimmy Dean, Why We Loved Him." *Movie Life*, September, 1956 and October, 1956.

**B076** Adams, Nick. "Hollywood's Mixed-Up Blabber-Mouths." *Screen Stars*, May 1957.

**B077** *The Advocate.* February 25, 1976.

Article focuses on questions of James Dean's alleged homosexuality, and reprints the views of Dean's friend Bill Bast, who believed that Dean was basically heterosexually oriented, but "he dabbled in everything."

**B078** Agan, Patrick. "James Dean: The Rebel Who Wouldn't Die." *Hollywood Studio Magazine*, August 1982.

A basic retread of career highlights and "voice of a generation" proselytizing. One of many articles on Dean in this tribute issue of *Hollywood Studio Magazine*.

**B079** Alexander, Paul. "Cause Without a Rebel." *Premiere*, September 1993, pp 80-82.

An excerpt from Alexander's Dean biography *Boulevard of Broken Dreams*.

**B080** Andrews, Rena. "Director Bridges is no Rebel, But Has a Cause in James Dean. *Denver Post*, October 16, 1977.

James Bridges, writer and director of the film *September 30, 1955*, recalls his own youthful fascination with James Dean.

**B081** Archerd, Army. *Variety*, October 3, 1955.

"It's still hard to believe the quick, tragic passing of James Dean," wrote legendary *Variety* columnist Army Archerd about the legend-to-be James Dean.

**B082** Ashenden, Larry. "Did Jimmy Dean Leave a Son?" *On the QT*, July 1957, pp 19-21, 65.

Details of "a persistent story coming out of Hollywood," claiming that Dean fathered a car-hop's baby shortly before he died. The woman is identified only as Mary B.

**B083** Astrachan, Sam. "The New Lost Generation." *The New Republic*, February 4, 1957, p. 17.

An insightful examination of the James Dean movie persona, that suggests he may have been more one-dimensional that critics believed, and describes the Dean cult as "silly and artificial." Several letters protesting the article appeared in the magazine's February 18 issue.

**B084**  Babitz, Eve. "They Might Be Giants." *Esquire*, May 1992, pp 118-121, 133.

Is Jason Priestley, Dana Ashbrook, or Jamie Walters the new James Dean? An interesting look at how young stars of the 1990's feel about being compared to Dean.

**B085**  Babuscio, Jack. "James Dean--A Gay Riddle." *Gay News*, #79.

The conclusion that James Dean was gay is inescapable, according to this article, that chides Dean biographers for not acknowledging this fact.

**B086**  Baker, Wayne. "The Girls Who Worship the Corpse of James Dean!" *Top Secret*, April 1961, pp 7, 39.

Sensational, hyperbole-laden account of "female fanatics" who "are still killing themselves in Dean's memory," and "are giving their bodies to any man who even resembles the pouting, surly, late star!"

**B087**  Bast, Bill. "There Was a Boy." *Photoplay*, September, October and November, 1956.

A lengthy excerpt from Bill Bast's biography of James Dean was featured in a three-part *Photoplay* article, which provides ample evidence that Bast's book, now almost impossible to find, remains one of the best Dean biographies ever written.

**B088**  Bean, Robin. "Dean: Ten Years After." *Films and Filming*, October 1965.

Basic career review, that includes some fine Dean commentary by director Francois Truffaut.

**B089**  Beata, Abby. "Did Jimmy Dean Commit Suicide?" *Anything Goes*, May 1956, pp 12-14.

Tabloid speculation that a depressed, insecure, death-obsessed Dean took his own life.

**B090**  *The Best of James Dean in the Scandal Magazines*, 1955-1958. Shake Publishing.

One-shot magazine that compiles the most outlandish of the tabloid articles written about James Dean.

**B091**  Bluttman, Susan. "Rediscovering James Dean: The TV Legacy." *Emmy* Magazine, September/October 1990, pp 50-56.

One of the best articles covering Dean's television appearances is this *Emmy* Magazine cover story, though it lists only those programs in which he played a significant role. Susan Bluttman was the co-curator of the 1986 James Dean television retrospective produced by the Museum of Broadcasting in New York.

**B092**  Browne, David. "James Dean Knew He Had a Date With Death!" *Confidential*, January 1958, pp 13, 46.

Uninspired rehash of the oft-told rumor that Dean had a death wish.

**B093**  Burr, Ty. "The First Rebel Yell." *Entertainment Weekly*, October 29, 1993, p. 50.

Fine essay on the filming of *Rebel Without a Cause*.

**B094**  *Campus USA*. "James Dean Alive on Campus." Spring 1988.

**B095**  Capen, Jeanne Balch. "The Strange Revival of James Dean." *The American Weekly*, July 29, 1956, pp 5-6.

One of many articles on Dean's post-mortem popularity, that draws a comparison between Dean and Rudolph Valentino.

**B096**  Carter, Lynne. "I Was a Friend of Jimmy Dean." *Rave*. January 1957, pp 30-35.

The opportunistic Lynne Carter, who was at best a casual acquaintance of Dean during his years in New York, tried many times to use the "relationship" to further her own career. This fanciful article is accompanied by numerous cheesecake photos of Carter.

**B097**  Carter, Lynne. "I Learned About Love from Jimmy Dean." *Rave*, April 1957, pp 24-27.

Lynne Carter's second attempt (see B096) to capitalize on the post-mortem James Dean craze.

**B098**  *Celebrity*. "Jimmy Dean: Why He Spits in Hollywood's Eye." December 1955.

"As far as some people are concerned, James Dean is one of the screwiest characters ever to stumble into the movies," begins this demeaning article that dismisses Dean as a poor man's Marlon Brando.

**B099**  Chastain, Sue. "The Hero Whose Cult Lives On." *Philadelphia Inquirer*, December 2, 1983.

"Why is Dean as popular with 16-year-olds in 1983 as he was in 1955?" is the question asked to adolescents in this piece.

**B100**  Christon, Lawrence. "Seeing Ourselves in James Dean." *Los Angeles Times*, September 29, 1985, p. 2.

"James Dean is still alive in a fathomlessly disturbing way," writes Christon in this heartfelt essay about how the struggle for identity shared by Dean's onscreen characters has continued to have an impact on audiences 30 years after his death.

**B101**  Christopher, Wendy. "The Star that Jimmy Dean and Elvis Presley Made." *Suppressed*, April 1957.

Cruel article about Natalie Wood, that accuses her of "climbing on the Dean wagon" after his death, and "putting words in his mouth to help her own career."

**B102**  Clemens, Harry. "The Romance That James Dean Couldn't Kill." *Uncensored*, March 1957, pp 35-37.

The relationship between Dean and Maila Nurmi is the focus of this inaccurate tabloid article.

**B103**  Clement, Hal. "The Man Who Freed Pier Angeli of James Dean's Ghost!" *Top Secret*, April 1962, pp 10-12.

Tabloid article alleging that Pier Angeli was "obsessed" by love for the late James Dean, until she met Christian Peuzet, a Frenchman described as Dean's double. Peuzet, shown in a photo, actually bears only a slight resemblance to Dean.

**B104**  Connolly, Mike. "This Was My Friend Jimmy Dean." *Modern Screen*, December 1955.

**B105**  Cooper, Dennis. "James Dean." *The Reader*, October 1, 1982.

An interesting piece accompanied by several photos, that compares Dean to everyone from poet Arthur Rimbaud to singer Darby Crash of the rock group The Germs.

**B106**  *Coronet*. "The Strange James Dean Death Cult." November 1956.

**B107**  Covert, Colin. "James Dean Still a Hero after 30 years." *Minneapolis Tribune*, September 30, 1985.

One of the better articles commemorating the 30th anniversary of Dean's death, covering Dean's global impact and his marketing resurrection.

**B108**  Dalton, David. "The Making of a Celluloid Rebel." *Rolling Stone*, June 20, 1974, pp 47-58.

Dean appears on the cover of *Rolling Stone*; the article is an excerpt from David Dalton's book *James Dean: The Mutant King*.

**B109**  Dalton, David. "How James Dean Came of Age on TV." *Village Voice*, March 4, 1986, pp 27-28.

Fine overview of James Dean's television work by David Dalton, author of two Dean biographies. The article was written to promote a retrospective of Dean's network performances at New York's Museum of Broadcasting.

**B110**  Dean, Emma Woolen. "James Dean: The Boy I Loved." *Photoplay*, March 1956, pp 57, 84-85.

Dean's grandmother, Emma Woolen Dean, recalls the last family reunion that Jimmy attended, and other memories of his childhood. Highly recommended.

**B111**  de Benedictis, Michel. "James Dean: The Rebel, His Cause and Effects." *New Orleans Review*, Fall/Winter 1984. pp 95-101.

"The questions that surround the emergence and establishment of cultural heroes are answerable only by a close examination of the society that creates them," writes de Benedictis in this scholarly article on the role of the rebel hero in society, as personified by James Dean.

**B112**  De Kolbe, Robert. "James Dean Speaks From the Grave." *True Strange*.

An interview with psychic Anna M. Van Deusen, who spoke to the deceased Dean in a seance.

**B 1 1 3** *Dig.* "James Dean." April 1957.

**B 1 1 4** *Dig.* "The Life of James Dean." November 1957.

**B 1 1 5** *Dig.* "The Miracle of James Dean." August 1962.

**B 1 1 6** *Dig.* "The James Dean Story: A Legend Revisited." August 1962.

**B 1 1 7** Dos Passos, John. "The Death of James Dean." *Esquire*, October 1958, pp 157,158, 384.

Free-form essay by short-story writer John Dos Passos; "James Dean is three years dead but the sinister adolescent still holds the headlines."

**B 1 1 8** Dufy, Lisette. "The Other Man in Vic Damone-Pier Angeli's LIfe!" *Behind The Scene*, January 1957, pp 10-12.

Tabloid history of the James Dean-Pier Angeli romance, that suggests Angeli still loves Dean even after marrying Vic Damone.

**B 1 1 9** Elliot, David. "30 Years Later, James Dean's Ghost Still Lives." *San Diego Union*, September 30, 1985.

Average 30th anniversary article, one of dozens that ran in newspapers across the country on September 30, 1985.

**B 1 2 0** *Elvis and Jimmy.* 1956.

One-shot magazine that explores the connections between Elvis Presley and James Dean.

**B 1 2 1** *Exposed.* "James Dean: The God of a Weird and Morbid Death Cult." September 1956, pp 10-15,56,57.

A surprisingly accurate biography of Dean, though the title of the article has little to do with its contents.

**B 1 2 2** *Fairmount News.* "James Dean First Place Winner in Dramatic Speaking." April 14, 1949.

The first time James Dean's name appeared in a newspaper was on the front page of his hometown *Fairmount News*.

**B123** *Films and Filming.* May 1964.

An interview with Elia Kazan, in which the director talks extensively about James Dean. While acknowledging his prodigious talent, Kazan also states, "I was never very appreciative of Jimmy Dean becoming an idol, he's not an idol of mine, and I didn't particularly like what he was."

**B124** *Films and Filming.* "The Dean Myth." January 1957.

**B125** *Films and Filming.* "Dean, Ten Years After." October 1965.

**B126** *Films and Filming.* "James Dean: The Rebel Saint 30 Years On." September 1985.

**B127** *Films Illustrated.* "Beloved Rebel." June 1976, pp 391-393.

Reverential article, which compares the first viewing of *Rebel Without a Cause* with the news of John F. Kennedy's assassination as a "common point of reference of a generation."

**B128** *Frauds.* "Why Hollywood Made a Saint of James Dean." April 1957, pp 63-65.

Article that inaccurately concludes that Dean "did not become a full-fledged matinee idol until after his tragic death."

**B129** Geller, J.S. "The Strange Life and Death of England's James Dean Cultist." *On the QT*, January 1963, pp 34-35, 52.

Tabloid article on Douglas Gordon Goodall, who changed his name legally to James Dean not long after Dean's death. In 1963, Goodall was found dead in his truck in the Brockley section of London.

**B130** Gilmore, John. "James Dean: The Rebel Recalled." *Gallery*, April 1974, pp 105-108.

John Gilmore is the author of the biography *The Real James Dean* and some of the more sensational articles about Dean's sexual preferences, including this one, which also describes in frank language Dean's slovenly manner and ambitious nature.

**B131** Goodman, Ezra. "Delirium Over Dead Star." *Life*, September 24, 1956, pp 75-76.

"Moviegoers are in a morbid craze for the late James Dean," writes Ezra Goodman. Article includes an interview with George Stevens, coverage of the first marketing wave surrounding Dean, and one of the most famous Dean-related quotes, Humphrey Bogart's belief that Dean "died at just the right time. If he had lived, he'd never have been able to live up to his publicity." First-rate.

**B132** Gore, Christian. *Film Threat: September 30, 1955, Never Happened.* 1988.

One-shot magazine about James Dean.

**B133** Gotram, Mike. "Did James Dean Commit Suicide?" *Hush-Hush*, January 1957, pp 13-17.

Article that blames Dean's "suicide" on his being rejected by Pier Angeli and Ursula Andress.

**B134** Guiley, Rosemary Ellen. "The Chilling Curse of James Dean's Death Car." *National Enquirer*, November 24, 1992.

This tabloid story alleges that the 1955 Porsche Spyder in which Dean died was "cursed," and vanished after causing "injury, death and mishap" to everyone who came in contact with it.

**B135** Guilliatt, Richard. "Rebel Within A Clause." *20/20*, March 1990.

This article on "Heaven's high earners," which includes James Dean, reports that there is "still a burgeoning black-market trade in chunks and paint flakes from the mangled Porsche."

**B136** Hadley, Richard. "The Myth That Was (and is) James Dean." *New York Post*, February 8, 1986.

On the day James Dean would have turned 55, Dean fan Richard Hadley tries to correct some long-held misconceptions about the legendary rebel hero.

**B137** Haspiel, James Robert. "The Legendary James Dean." *Hollywood Studio Magazine*, August 1982.

Provocative quotes about Dean from Shelley Winters are the highlight of this piece.

**B138** Haskell, Molly. "Rebel With a Shrine." *Vogue*, September 1988.

"I was never drawn to candle-burning, but the fanaticism surrounding Dean I can understand," writes Haskell in this touching tribute.

**B139** Hoffman, Jim. "Can Dean Stockwell Shake Off the Jimmy Dean Jinx?" *Photoplay*, November 1958.

Comparisons between James Dean and Dean Stockwell were common in the late 1950's, especially after Stockwell experienced a near-fatal car accident.

**B140** *Hollywood Reporter.* "Princeton Honors Dean." March 1, 1956.

**B141** *Hollywood Reporter.* "Warners Claim to Dean Name, Image Rejected." July 17, 1992.

A judge ruled that Dean's 1954 contract with Warner Bros. does not give the studio the merchandising rights to the star's image. Warners claimed it has lost over $30 million in revenue as a result of the sales of Dean memoribilia by Curtis Management, the company authorized by the Dean family to license the actor's image.

**B142** *Hollywood Studio Magazine.* "James Dean Tribute." May 1982.

**B143** *Hollywood Studio Magazine.* "Sal Mineo and James Dean: Their Secret Friendship." September 1986.

**B144** *Hollywood Studio Magazine.* "The James Dean Dedication." March 1989.

**B145** Honor, Elizabeth. "Hollywood Tragedies." *Cosmopolitan*, October 1956.

Profiles of "the brilliant, the beautiful, the talented--who came to Hollywood seeking success and happiness and glory; but for some, it was an appointment with death." Among those profiled with Dean are Jean Harlow, John Gilbert and Lupe Velez.

**B146** Hopper, Hedda. "Keep Your Eye on James Dean." *Chicago Tribune*, March 27, 1955.

This article is mentioned in almost every biography of James Dean, and has become one of the most famous examples of the "Rebel"'s ability to play the Hollywood game with the best of them. Powerful gossip columnist Hedda Hopper was unimpressed with James Dean at first, whom she derisively refers to as "the young genius in our midst," but after Dean showed up on time at Hopper's home, wearing a suit and patiently answering questions about his childhood and his career goals, Hedda became one of Dean's most vocal supporters.

B147  Hopper, Hedda. "Young Men of Hollywood." *Coronet*, June 1955.

B148  Hopper, Hedda. "Young Men of Hollywood, Pt. 2." *Coronet*, July 1955.

B149  Hudson, Rock. "The Truth About Liz Taylor, Jimmy Dean and Me." *Movie Stars Parade*. March 1962.

B150  Huizenga, Chris. "James Dean and Ferment in the Fifties." *After Dark*, February 1976.

Biogarphy and career review, with excerpts from the biography *James Dean: The Mutant King*.

B151  Hunt, Evelyn. "To James Dean." *Photoplay*, January 1956, p. 51.

A letter and poem to James Dean written by Vermont school teacher Evelyn Hunt, who goes to movies "as an escape from a strenuous schedule." "No one else's death has ever affected me in quite the same way (as Dean's)," she writes.

B152  Hutchings, Harold. "The Woman Behind James Dean." *Chicago Tribune*, March 3, 1957, p.20

Interview with Adeline Nall about Dean's interest in acting while he was a student in grammar school.

B153  Hyams, Joe. "James Dean." *Redbook*, September 1956.

B154  *Inside*. "The Unvarnished Truth About James Dean." April 1957, pp 60-64.

Article that sets out to prove what Jimmy Dean's fanatical followers "seem unable to accept; 1. he *is* dead. 2. his body lays in an Indiana grave. 3. his untimely death was purely accidental."

**B155**  *Inside Story.* "The Amazing James Dean Hoax!" February 1957,
pp 45-49.

Amusing conspiracy theory about four Warner Bros. executives who met
in secret to outline a scheme to cash in on James Dean's death.

**B156**  *Interview*, March 1972.

Twenty-seven photos of James Dean are the highlight of this *Interview*
cover story.

**B157**  *The James Dean Album.* 1956.

One-shot magazine, published by Ideal.

**B158**  *James Dean: The Man and the Legend.* 1988.

British one-shot magazine published by SM Distribution.

**B159**  *Jimmy Dean Returns!* 1956.

"Read his own words from beyond!" promised this one-shot magazine
devoted to Dean, published by *Rave* Magazine.

**B160**  Jones, Wayne. "James Dean. . .25 years later." *Goldmine*,
January 1981, p.20.

Article focuses on the 25th anniversary tribute to Dean organized by
actor Martin Sheen and Dean's former teacher Adeline Nall.

**B161**  Kart, Larry. "Giant Legacy: The Hero That James Dean Created
Still Lives." *Chicago Tribune*, September 15, 1985.

One of the most objective articles written at or around the 30th
anniversary of James Dean's death. Tribune film critic Larry Kart calls
Dean's work in *Giant* " a ridiculous performance in many ways," but
describes *Rebel Without a Cause* as "a landmark in American movie
history."

**B162**  Keller, Julia. "Mythic Hero in America's Heartland." *America*, 1977,
pp 4-6.

Directions to and recommendations for a trip to James Dean's grave in Fairmount, Indiana.

**B163** Kendall, Robert. "James Dean Collecting is Now World-Wide." *Hollywood Studio Magazine*, August 1982.

Coverage on the popularity of James Dean merchandise in Japan and Europe.

**B164** Kilbanoff, Hank. "James Dean: After 30 Years, His Cause Still Draws Fans to his Hoosier Hometown." *Washington Post*, September 30, 1985.

The Fairmount celebrations that marked the 30th anniversary of James Dean's death, and the people who attended, are the subject of this piece.

**B165** Korman, Seymour. "The Last Hour of James Dean." *Chicago Tribune*, February 5, 1956.

Overdramatic but generally accurate account of Dean's ill-fated drive to Salinas.

**B166** *The Late James Dean*. 1983.

One-shot British publication.

**B167** Leonard, William. "Hoosier Hometowns Re-Live James Dean's Story." *Chicago Tribune*, September 26, 1957.

Coverage of the opening of the documentary *The James Dean Story* in Marion, Indiana.

**B168** *Life* Magazine. "Moody New Star." March 7, 1955. pp 125-128.

One of the first major features written about James Dean, featuring the famous Dennis Stock photo of Dean walking through New York's Times Square in the rain.

**B169** Lindahl, John. "My Death Drive With James Dean." *On the QT*, March 1958, pp 22-23, 64.

An article that purports to tell, for the first time, Rolf Wutherich's account of his journey with James Dean, and the fatal crash.

**B170**  *Look*. "These Will Be the Brightest New Stars of 1955." January 11, 1955.

One of the first national magazine articles to notice James Dean's potential; "He will be the most dynamic discovery since Marlon Brando."

**B171**  *Los Angeles Times*. "Jimmy Dean Says He Isn't Flattered by Being Labeled 'Another Brando.'" November 7, 1954.

One of the first articles devoted to James Dean in a major newspaper.

**B172**  *Los Angeles Times*. "From the James Dean Archives." July 7, 1985.

**B173**  *Los Angeles Times*. "Dean Ruling." April 8, 1993. p.F2

Story about the court judgment against Warner Bros. studios for illegally using James Dean's name and likeness.

**B174**  Loynd, Ray. "Some Unsentimental Memories of James Dean by Rock Hudson." *Hollywood Reporter*, August 9, 1968.

Actor Rock Hudson alleges that Dean "hated George Stevens, and was always angry and full of contempt," during the shooting of *Giant*.

**B175**  Marlowe, Derek. "Soliloquy on James Dean's Forty-Fifth Birthday." *New York*, November 8, 1976, pp 41-43.

"When Dean was killed and *Rebel Without a Cause* was released, the farm boy from Indiana was elected hero by his generation," writes Marlowe in this excellent biography and career assessment. Accompanying the article is an artist's conception of what Dean would look like at the age of 45.

**B176**  Mathews, Lou. "Highway 46 Revisited." *Los Angeles Weekly*, September 27, 1985, pp 27-28.

An examination of James Dean's final drive through Cholame, California, and how the city rememberes the actor on the anniversary of his death.

**B177**  Maychick, Diana. "James Dean's Still a Giant." *New York Post*, September 23, 1985.

An interview with Dean superfan David Loehr, and Linda Malcolm, who organized a James Dean retrospective for Warner Bros..

**B178** McCarthy, Jim. "It's Me, Jimmy." *Modern Screen*, December 1956.

**B179** McCollum, Charlie. "Is Dean Tribute Much Ado About Nearly Nothing?" *Washington Star*, September 21, 1975, p E4.

"Rarely has so much been made of so little," writes McCollum about the American Film Institute tribute to James Dean, though he acknowledges that Dean's performance in *Rebel Without a Cause* was "a symbol of 1950's youth that may well endure for all time."

**B180** Mellor, William C.. "The James Dean I Knew." *Picturegoer*, December 29, 1956.

William C. Mellor was the cinematographer on the film *Giant*.

**B181** Millen, Roger. "Was James Dean a Psycho?" *On the QT*, March 1957.

"Hysterical teenagers have made a hero of Dean. But Hollywood insiders who knew him like a book say 'He was a bum,'" according to this dubious tabloid expose`.

**B182** Mineo, Sal. "I Still Remember James Dean." *TV and Movie Screen*, November 1959.

**B183** *Modern Screen*. "Smoldering Dynamite." June 1955.

**B184** *Modern Screen*. "Lone Wolf." August 1955.

**B185** *Modern Screen*. "The Secret Love that Haunts Jimmy Dean." October 1955.

**B186** *Modern Screen*. "The Last Story About Jimmy." October 1955.

**B187** *Modern Screen*. "Appointment With Death." December 1955.

**B188** *Modern Screen*. "Goodbye, Jimmy." March 1956.

**B189** *Modern Screen*. "Your James Dean Memorial Medallion." October 1956.

**B190** *Modern Screen.* "Jimmy Dean's Last Message." January 1957.

**B191** *Modern Screen.* "His Love Destroyed Him." February 1957.

**B192** *Modern Screen.* "Was Jimmy Dean's Sports Car Jinxed?" February 1957.

**B193** *Modern Screen.* "What Jimmy Dean Believed." October 1957.

**B194** *Motion Picture Magazine.* "Jimmy Dean Is Not Dead." May 1956.

**B195** *Motion Picture Magazine.* "James Dean, His Life and Loves." September 1956.

**B196** *Motion Picture Magazine.* "The Ghost Who Wrecked Pier Angeli's Marriage." February 1959.

**B197** *Motion Picture Magazine.* "Where is Jimmy Dean?" May 1961.

**B198** *Movieland.* "Dean's Big Balk." November 1955.

**B199** *Movieland.* "Man of Many Moods." November 1955.

**B200** *Movieland.* "The Star Who Never Died." October 1956.

**B201** *Movieland.* "How Jimmy Dean Still Works Miracles For Others." December 1956.

**B202** *Movieland.* "Jean-Paul Belmondo, He's the French James Dean." December 1962.

**B203** *Movieland.* "Elvis Hears from James Dean." August 1963.

**B204** *Movie Life.* "Daffy About Dean." November 1955.

**B205** *Movie Life.* "The Untold Story of James Dean's Last Days." December 1955.

**B206** *Movie Life.* "The Movie Life of James Dean." January 1956.

**B207** *Movie Life.* "Jimmy Dean Fights Back From the Grave." June 1956.

**B208** *Movie Life.* "James Dean's Strange Legacy." July 1956.

**B209** *Movie Life.* "Secrets From Jimmy Dean's Past." July 1956.

**B210** *Movie Life.* "The Secret Happiness of Jimmy Dean." August 1956.

**B211** *Movie Life.* "The Untold Story of the Love Jimmy Lost." January 1957.

**B212** *Movie Life.* "Should Elvis Presley Play Jimmy Dean?" January 1957.

**B213** *Movie Life.* "Will They Cheat Jimmy Again?" February 1957.

**B214** *Movie Life.* "What You Owe Jimmy Dean." May 1957.

**B215** *Movie Life.* "Why They Want You to Forget Jimmy." July 1957.

**B216** *Movie Life.* "In Loving Memory: James Dean." September 1957.

**B217** *Movie Life.* "News from Dean Foundation." October 1957.

**B218** *Movie Life.* "Did Jimmy Dean's Spirit Haunt the Studio?" October 1957.

**B219** *Movie Life.* "James Dean: Three Years of Sorrow, Never Forgotten, Never Replaced." October 1958.

**B220** *Movie Life.* "James Dean--Pier Angeli." April 1962.

**B221** *Movie Stars Parade.* "What Jimmy Dean Did to Hollywood." September 1955.

**B222** *Movie Stars Parade.* "The Strange Lovemaking of Jimmy Dean." October 1955.

**B223** *Movie Stars Parade.* "The Deepening Mystery of Jimmy Dean." April 1956.

**B224** *Movie Stars Parade.* "The Boy Who Didn't Die." May 1956.

**B225** *Movie Stars Parade.* "His Living Legacy, His Searching Part." May 1956.

**B226** *Movie Stars Parade.* "What Made Jimmy Run?" May 1956.

**B227** *Movie Stars Parade.* "The Real Jimmy Dean." May 1956.

**B228** *Movie Stars Parade.* "Those Who Loved Him." May 1956.

**B229** *Movie Stars Parade.* "As You Remember Him." June 1956.

**B230** *Movie Stars Parade.* "Secrets From Jimmy Dean's Past." July 1956.

**B231** *Movie Stars Parade.* "What Jimmy Dean's Hometown Can Now Reveal." August 1956.

**B232** *Movie Stars Parade.* "Must We Stop Writing About Jimmy Dean?" December 1956.

**B233** *Movie Stars Parade.* "Jimmy Dean's Fight to Live." February 1957.

**B234** *Movie Stars Parade.* "James Dean's Memorial Page." April 1957, May 1957.

**B235** *Movie Stars Parade.* "Is Natalie Wood Betraying Jimmy Dean?" June 1957.

**B236** *Movie Stars Parade.* "James Dean: The Tragedy Lives On." August 1957.

**B237** *Movie Stars Parade.* "Six Unsolved Mysteries of Jimmy Dean's Death." October 1958.

**B238** Nakao, Annie. "Coming by the Carload to Honor Dean." *Los Angeles Herald-Examiner*, September 28, 1981.

Coverage of the James Dean Memorial Rally and other Dean-related events in Cholame, California.

**B239** Nelson, Lori. "The Dean I've Dated." *Modern Screen*, September 1955.

**B240** Nerad, Jack R. "On the Trail of James Dean." *Motor Trend*, September 1985, pp 62-64, 67.

A retracing of the Dean death-route in a vintage Porsche 550 Spyder. The article will be of greater interest to automobile buffs than Dean fans.

**B241** *Newsweek.* "Transition." October 10, 1955.

Obituary of a "one-time law student actor, whose portrayal of a brooding, inarticulate adolescent in the movie *East of Eden* rocketed him to stardom."

**B242** *Newsweek.* "Stars That Won't Dim." June 18, 1956.

Article notes how photos, sculptures and memoribilia of James Dean is outselling that of any living star, and chronicles the emergence of more than 50 highly active Dean fan clubs.

**B243** *New Yorker.* "Fan." August 2, 1969.

A story about Mrs. Therese J. Brandes, the founder and president of the James Dean Memory Club, who "has given all the time that she could spare, and a good deal that she couldn't, to preserving the memory of James Dean."

**B244** *New York Times.* "Of Local Origin." March 6, 1954.

Coverage of the announcement made by Elia Kazan's office that James Dean has been signed to play Cal Trask in *East of Eden.*

**B245** *New York Times.* "James Dean's Estate Sued." August 23, 1956.

News story about the $100,000 lawsuit filed against the estate of James Dean by Rolf Wutherich, who charged Dean was driving too fast and with "wanton disregard" for the safety of his passenger.

**B246** *New York Times.* "Tribute to Actor Starts TV 'War'". October 4, 1956.

The battle between Ed Sullivan and Steve Allen over scheduled James Dean tributes on their respective shows is chronicled.

**B247** *New York Times.* "Two James Dean Grants Given to Young Actors." July 26, 1951.

Richard Kutney and Leon Embry became the first recipients of James Dean Scholarships to the Neighborhood Playhouse School in New York City.

**B248** Nielsen, Evelyn Washburn. "The Truth About James Dean."

*Chicago Tribune*, September 9, 1956.

Inteviews with Marcus and Ortense Winslow and several of their Fairmount, Indiana neighbors. Recommended.

**B249** O'Dowd, Brian. *Hollywood Studio Magazine*. August 1982, pp 12-14.

One of several articles in this special tribute issue to James Dean, consisting of a biographical sketch and comments from numerous friends and coworkers.

**B250** O'Dowd, Brian. "The James Dean Dedication." *Hollywood Studio Magazine*, pp 16-17.

Coverage of the unveiling of the James Dean memorial at Griffith Observatory, attended by several *Rebel Without a Cause* cast members and artist Kennth Kendall.

**B251** O'Dowd, Brian. "Studio Co-Workers Remember Dean." *Hollywood Studio Magazine*, August 1982.

**B252** O'Toole, Lawrence. "Saint James: Rebel Without Claws." *Us* Magazine, October 15, 1990.

Excellent story about Dean's rebel image that contains many memorable quotes, including John Waters' observation that "A bad attitude is the ultimate beauty mark," and "A smirk from a Dean photo is like a stamp that says 'Made in the USA.'"

**B253** *The Official James Dean Anniversary Book*. 1956.

One-shot magazine devoted to James Dean, edited by Peter Meyerson and published by Dell.

**B254** Owen, Gene. "An Unforgettable Day With Jimmy Dean." *Movieland*, February 1957.

**B255** Owen, Gene Nielson. "The Man Who Would Be 50: A Memory of James Dean." *Los Angeles Times*, February 8, 1981.

Gene Owen, James Dean's teacher and counselor at Santa Monica City College, recalls how she tried to help Dean overcome his "Hoosier accent," and how he practiced by reading soliloquies from *Hamlet*.

Recommended.

**B256**  *Palm Beach Post*. "James Dean: Keeping the Faithful." October 7, 1990.

Above-average article on Marion and Fairmount, Indiana, 35 years after Dean's death.

**B257**  *Paris Match*. "Les Immortels." July 19, 1985.

James Dean, Marilyn Monroe, Humphrey Bogart and John Wayne are profiled.

**B258**  Parsons, Louella. "James Dean--New Face With Future." *Cosmopolitan*, March 1955, p. 44.

"This month in *East of Eden*, you will see a young actor. . .who, we predict, is going to be more than a meteor in the Hollywood sky," writes gossip columnist Louella Parsons.

**B259**  Parsons, Louella. "I Nominate For Stardom." *Modern Screen*, March 1955.

**B260**  Parsons, Louella. "Jim Dean's Funeral." *Modern Screen*, January 1956.

**B261**  *People*. "Obsessed by James Dean, Japan's Seita Onishi Makes a Monument to That Fallen Rebel His Cause." August 7, 1989.

Japanese millionaire Seita Onishi's quest to build a Wall of Hope sculpture in Paris, dedicated to James Dean, is the subject of this article.

**B262**  *People*. "James Dean's Hometown Revels Without Pause in Fond Memory of Fairmount's Favorite Son." October 15, 1990, pp 114-115.

Brief, photo-laden article on the preparations in Fairmount, Indiana to commemorate the 35th anniversary of James Dean's death.

**B263**  *People*. "Like Jim Morrison, Working Stiffs from Elvis to Marilyn Are Still Striking It Rich." March 18, 1991.

According to this story about the merchandising of dead celebrities, consumers spend $3 million annually on James Dean posters, t-shirts and other items.

**B264**  *People.* "James Dean." July 27, 1992.

In a special double-issue devoted to teen idols, Dean is described as "a tarnished angel whose brooding presence hinted at trouble."

**B265**  *Personal Romances.* "I Was Jimmy Dean's Wife." April 1959, pp 23,52-56.

"You probably won't believe this story, and I don't much care whether you do or not, but I just have to get it out of my system," is the first line of this impassioned letter/article from an unnamed woman who claims to have married Dean in Tijuana.

**B266**  Peterson, Iver. "Young Drawn to James Dean 25 Years After." *New York Times*, October 1, 1980.

The 25th anniversary of Dean's death is the topic of this article, which features interviews with several Dean cult members.

**B267**  Petit, Chris. "Live Fast, Die Young." *Time Out*, September 26, 1975.

An article written to commemorate the 20th anniversary of James Dean's death; "James Dean was the first film star with whom a teenage generation could exclusively identify."

**B268**  *Premiere.* "James Dean." September 1993.

Obituary-like biography and filmography.

**B269**  *Private Lives.* "Is James Dean a Dandy?" October 1955, pp 52-54.

"What gives with the Dean lad?" asks this sleazy tabloid piece. "He isn't interested in dames and is definitely not offbeat, so what is his angle? Is Jamie uninterested, undersexed or immature or busy?"

**B270**  *Private Lives.* "Jimmy Dean's Alive!" June 1957, pp 36-44.

Uncommonly long expose, accompanied by a photo supposedly taken of Dean after his death, and the offer of a $50,000 reward for more information on his whereabouts.

**B271**  Raleigh, Joel. "The Girl James Dean Was Going to Marry!" *Lowdown*, May 1957, pp 17,62.

According to this tabloid piece, Dean was engaged to marry a Baton Rouge, Louisiana, girl named Betty Lou Simmons. However, since the article does not even report the day of Dean's death accurately, the story is almost certainly false.

**B272**  *Rave*. "Did James Dean Really Die?" May 1956, pp 24-27.

Tabloid tripe about "the luscious dolls Dean left behind, (who) won't let the handsome ghoul rest in peace."

**B273**  *Rave*. "James Dean Tells His Life Story 'In his Own Words'". November 1956.

Tabloid article pieced together by "quotes" from Dean, that are no more than speculations of unnamed "people who knew Dean" on what he might have said. Worthless.

**B274**  *Rave*. "Why Jimmy Won't Win Any Oscars" April 1957, pp 58-61.

A story that lambasts the Motion Picture Academy for "politicking, vote-bribing, dagger-tossing, flower-strewing," and a host of other crimes, all of which contributed to Dean not winning an Oscar. Ridiculous, but fun.

**B275**  *Rave*. "Why Jimmy Dean is a Living Lie." September 1957, pp 16-19.

"Hollywood's lover boy was more heel than hero," according to this vicious tabloid piece.

**B276**  *The Real James Dean Story*. 1956.

One-shot magazine published by Fawcett, and edited by Mary Callahan. Among the articles are remembrances written by Bob Hinkle, Hedda Hopper and Sal Mineo.

**B277**  Redifer, Rex. "Giant Crowd of Visitors Invade Actor's Hometown to Mark His Life, Death." *Indianapolis Star*, September 26, 1988.

On the 33rd anniversary of James Dean's death, the *Indianapolis Star* reports that over 30,000 people turned out in Fairmount, Indiana, to pay tribute.

**B278**  Rees, Robert, "I Was James Dean's Black Madonna." *Sh-Boom*,
          1989.

Dean fan Robert Rees interviews Maila Nurmi, the one-time Vampira and
friend of James Dean.

**B279**  Remington, Ann. "James Dean: The Tragedy That Lives On."
          *Movie Stars Parade*. August 1957, pp 33,60.

"Is there a jinx from the past that haunts the lives of those. . .who have
been touched by Jimmy?" asks Remington in this strange article.

**B280**  *Rocky Mountain News*. "Incredible Revival of James Dean Cult."
          March 16, 1975.

Well-done, surprisingly detailed biographical sketch.

**B281**  Roller, Alfred C.. "The James Dean Myth Blows Up." *New York
          World-Telegram*, November 3, 1956.

Interview with *Giant* director George Stevens, who decrys the myth-
making about James Dean as "ghoulish nonsense." "Jimmy was just a
regular kid trying to make good in Hollywood."  Stevens also discounts
the "death-wish" rumors surrounding Dean. "Jimmy lived fast and he died
fast. But one thing is sure. He didn't want to die."

**B282**  Rosenman, Leonard. "Jimmy Dean: Giant Legend, Cult Rebel."
          *Los Angeles Times*, December 18, 1977.

Dean's friend Leonard Rosenman recalls how Dean looked to him as a
father figure. Rosenman also writes about the music he composed for
James Bridges' film *September 30, 1955*.

**B283**  Roth, Sanford. "The Late James Dean." *Collier's*, November 25,
          1955.

Photographer and longtime Dean friend Sanford Roth was assigned by
*Collier's* to cover the car race in Salinas, California that was Dean's
destination on the day of his death. He penned this brief but moving
elegy to Dean, accompanied by several fine photographs.

**B284**  Roth, Sanford. "Jimmy Dean: The Assignment I'll Never Forget."
          *Popular Photography*, July 1962.

**B285**  Rowland, Steve. "Goodbye, Jimmy Dean." *Movie Stars Parade*, November 1957.

**B286**  Rykken, Rolf. "Friend's Play Marks Dean Anniversary." *Delaware State News*, February 15, 1976.

An article on Bill Bast's decision to break a long silence about his best friend by writing a television adaptation of his James Dean biography.

**B287**  Sassin, Richard. "Rebel Without a Band." *Music Connection*, October 28, 1985.

"John Lennon said 'Before Elvis there was nothing.' But Elvis knew that he owed a debt to James Dean." So begins this article that calls Dean "the first rock star."

**B288**  *Saturday Review*. "It's Dean, Dean, Dean." October 13, 1956.

A review of *Giant*, and the impact of James Dean's death on the film's reception.

**B289**  Schaeffer, Sam. "James Dean Vs. Elvis Presley." *Whisper*, December 1956. pp 15-17.

A compare-and-contrast article on the two most significant adolescent heroes of the 1950's. "After reading these summaries, we leave it to you to judge which idol--if either--you would rather have your own children worship."

**B290**  Schaeffer, Sam. "James Dean's Black Madonna." *Whisper*, February 1956, pp 12-16,.

A lurid profile of the "chilling, gruesome and macabre" relationship between Dean and Maila Nurmi.

**B291**  Schaeffer, Sam. "The Girl James Dean Left Behind." *Whisper*, August 1956, pp 8-11, 55.

Inaccurate, romanticized profile of Christine White, salvaged by a good selection of photos.

**B292**  Schaeffer, Sam. "How James Dean Got an Oscar." *Whisper*, February 1957, pp 53-54.

One of the more intriguing tabloid items, which contends that friends of James Dean had acquired Frank Sinatra'a Academy Award for "The House That I Live In," and presented it to Dean, who held on to it until his death. The problem--Frank Sinatra never won an Oscar for "The House That I Live In."

**B293** Schaeffer, Sam. "James Dean--The Ghost Drive of Polonio Pass." *Whisper*, December 1957.

In this darkly amusing tabloid piece, Schaeffer "investigates" rumors of a "phantom Porsche, racing through the night on the road to Paso Robles," but cannot confirm that Dean's spirit is at the wheel.

**B294** *Screen Greats Presents James Dean*. 1988.

One-shot magazine published by Starlog Press.

**B295** *Screen Legends: James Dean (His Life and Legend)*. 1965.

One-shot magazine, edited by Gene Ringgold and published by Associated Professional Services. Half the magazine was devoted to James Dean, and half to Carroll Baker.

**B296** *Screen Stars*. "The Immortal Dean." November 1956.

**B297** *Screen Stars*. "Leave Him to Heaven." March 1957.

**B298** *Screen Stories*. "The Unlighted Road: The Jimmy Dean Festival." September 1956.

**B299** *Screen Stories*. "Jimmy Dean, Two Memories." November 1956.

**B300** Scullin, George. "James Dean: The Legend and the Facts." *Look*, October 16, 1956, p. 122-128.

One of the best biographies and career reviews written in the aftermath of Dean's death, including several photos. Scullin examines the many manifestations of Dean's "strange posthumous fame."

**B301** Segaloff, Nat. "James Dean's Lasting Appeal." *Boston Herald*. September 30, 1990.

"The cult wanes but never completely fades," writes Nat Segaloff of James Dean's loyal following on the 35th anniversary of his death.

**B302**  *Seventeen.* "An Actor in Search of Himself." October 1955.

**B303**  Shaw, Bill. "Dead 25 Years, James Dean Is Given a Touching Hometown Tribute by Nostalgic Fans." *People*, October 13, 1980.

The article's title tells the story.

**B304**  Sheridan, Elizabeth. "In Memory of Jimmy." *Photoplay*, October 1957, pp 70, 102-105.

Excellent remembrance of Dean by Elizabeth "Dizzy" Sheridan, one of Dean's closest friends during his years in New York.

**B305**  *Sixteen Magzine.* "Jimmy the Kid!" March 1959.

**B306**  *Sixteen Magazine.* "A Tribute to Jimmy." September 1959.

**B307**  Skolsky, Sidney. "Demon Dean." *Photoplay*, July 1955, pp 38, 72-73.

Hollywood columnist Sidney Skolsky wrote this, the first of many outstanding articles on James Dean to appear in *Photoplay*. Skolsky interviewed Dean at Googie's Coffee Shop, the actor's favorite Hollywood hangout.

**B308**  St. Pierre, Roger. *James Dean: A Story in Words and Pictures.* 1985.

One-shot British magazine devoted to James Dean, published by Anabas Books.

**B309**  Stevens, George. "A Tenderness Lost." *Modern Screen*, January 1956.

**B310**  Stevens, George. *Cahiers Du Cinema*, July 1956.

**B311**  Stevens, George. "The Actor Jimmy Dean." *Screen Stories*, November 1956.

**B312**  Sullivan, Drew. "The Mysteries of James Dean." *Scarlet Street*, Winter 1995. pp 37, 40-41, 103.

"Four decades after his tragic death, James Dean is having one of the busiest years of his career," writes Sullivan in this comprehensive account of Dean-related books, movies and merchandising.

**B313** Taussig, Perry. "James Dean's Torrid Love Letters." *Lowdown*, January 1957, pp 29, 43.

Not letters written by Dean, but letters written to him after his death are the subject of this tabloid piece.

**B314** *Time*. "Milestones." October 10, 1955.

Obituary that describes Dean as the "most promising young cinemactor of 1955."

**B315** *Time*. "The Dean Cult." November 26, 1955.

Less than three months after Dean's death, *Time* was already covering "the weird posthumous cult of James Dean."

**B316** *Time*. "Dean of the One-Shotters." September 3, 1956.

An article that chronicles the Dean magazine phenomenon. Dozens of one-shot publications dedicated to Dean are selling thousands of copies every month."

**B317** Turnquist, Kristi. "Of James Dean and Immortality." *The Oregonian*, December 30, 1990.

"In the Dead Celebrity Hall of Fame, Dean occupies a well-tended shrine," according to this review of the book *James Dean: Behind the Scene*, which also assesses the status of the Dean mythos in 1990.

**B318** *TV and Movie Screen*. "Jimmy Dean, The Story He Wanted to Tell." September 1956.

**B319** *TV and Movie Screen*. "Jimmy Dean's Happiest Night." May 1957.

**B320** Tweedale, Tony. "The Legend of James Dean." *Photoplay*, June 1972, pp 54-56.

The eleventh installment of *Photoplay's* *Great Stars* series, and one of the few bios to mention Dean's three bit parts in movies before his casting in *East of Eden*.

**B321** *Uncensored.* "Those James Dean Whispers." September 1956, pp 44-47.

"Did he die for love? Or was it for 'kicks'?" asks this typical tabloid piece.

**B322** *Vanity Fair.* "James Dean." July 1994.

One-paragraph story about the "eternal teen," who is "poised for an image overhaul that might make Madonna swoon," after the release of Paul Alexander's Dean biography.

**B323** *Vogue.* "The Next Successes." February 1, 1955, pp 170-171.

"Eight Americans in the Arts" are profiled briefly, but only two--James Dean and Arthur Penn--lived up to the "Next Successes" label.

**B324** *Whisper.* "James Dean's Fans Speak Their Minds." April 1956, pp 44-45.

*Whisper* devoted two pages to letters from Dean fans, some supportive and others outraged.

**B325** Wills, Beverly. "I Almost Married Jimmy Dean. Who Am I?" *Modern Screen*, March 1957.

**B326** Wilmington, Michael. "James Dean: An Appreciation." *High Times*, April 1981.

Pompous, beat poet style prose adorns photos of James Dean by Dennis Stock.

**B327** Winslow, Marcus. "You Can Make Jimmy Dean Live Forever." *Modern Screen*, November 1956.

Article written by James Dean's uncle.

**B328** Wood, Natalie. "You Haven't Heard the Half About Jimmy!" *Photoplay*, November 1955, pp 55,82,84.

Fascinating article written before Dean's death by Natalie Wood, and published two months after the crash that ended Dean's life. Wood refutes rumors that Dean is "weird, sullen, or an oddball," and describes her first meeting with the actor, and their relationship while filming *Rebel Without a Cause*.

**B329** Wood, Natalie. "I Can't Forget Jimmy." *Movie Life*, December 1956.

**B330** Wood, Natalie. "Natalie Wood Reviews the James Dean Story." *Photoplay*, September 1957, pp 72, 102.

Natalie Wood expresses her belief that *The James Dean Story* "will please Jimmy Dean fans," and "as for people who can't understand why there still are Dean fans--now they'll know."

**B331** Worth, Frank. "Jimmy Told Me: Don't Print That Photo!" *Sixteen Magazine*, November 1957.

**B332** Wuntch, Philip. "James Dean: The legend endures." *Dallas Morning News*, September 29, 1985.

One of dozens of articles to appear on the 30th anniversary of Dean's death.

**B333** Wutherich, Rolf. "James Dean's Last Passenger Recovers--Tells Complete Story of Fateful Death Drive." *Modern Screen*, October 1957.

**B334** Yates, Brock. "Far From Eden." *Car and Driver*, October 1985, pp 85-90.

Outstanding, meticulously-detailed account of Dean's purchase of the Porsche Spyder, the route he drove on his final day, and the fate of the car and those connected to it in the aftermath.

**B335** Zahn, Debra. "James Dean: Rebel With an Agent." *Los Angeles Times*, September 29, 1985, pp3, 42.

"For 30 years the name and likeness of James Dean have lived in the hearts of fans. Now, they are up for sale," writes Zahn in this entertaining look at how Dean's image has been marketed.

**B336** Zavatsky, William. "Reflections on the Life and Death of James Dean." *Rolling Stone*, October 16, 1980, pp 50-53.

Author Zavatsky recalls the impact that the films of James Dean had on him during his own adolesence.

# 8

# AWARDS AND HONORS

With the exception of A1, all awards are posthumous.

**A 1**  **The Daniel Blum Theatre World Award** (1954). James Dean was one of eleven young stage performers to be singled out as the "Most Promising Personalities" of the 1954 season, for his work in *The Immoralist* (see S9). Other winners include Eva Marie Saint, Harry Belafonte, Ben Gazzara and Elizabeth Montgomery.

**A 2**  **Best Actor nomination** (1955). Dean was nominated for his performance as Cal Trask in *East of Eden*. He lost to Ernest Borgnine in *Marty*.

**A 3**  **Best Performance by a Male Star** (1955). *Film Daily* magazine honored five actors with its "Best Performance" award; James Dean (*East of Eden*), Ernest Borgnine (*Marty*), James Cagney (*Love Me or Leave Me*), Henry Fonda (*Mr. Roberts*) and Spencer Tracy (*Bad Day at Black Rock*).

**A 4**  **Finds of the Year** (1955). Five performers were chosen by *Film Daily* magazine as 1955's most promising new faces; James Dean (*East of Eden*), Ernest Borgnine (*Marty*), Fess Parker (*Davy Crockett*), Julie Harris (*I Am a Camera*), Dana Wynter (*The View From Pompey's Head*).

**A 5**  **Stars of Tomorrow** (1955). The Motion Picture Exhibitors ranked ten performers in its annual list of "Stars of Tomorrow." Dean placed at number six, preceded by Jack Lemmon, Tab

Hunter, Dorothy Malone, Kim Novak and Ernest Borgnine. Rounding out the list are Anne Francis, Richard Egan, Eva Marie Saint and Russ Tamblyn.

**A6**  **Best Actor** (1955). The first-annual Audience Awards Election, held on December 6, 1955 at the Beverly Hilton Hotel, honored the best performances of the years as voted by moviegoers across the nation. Fifteen million ballots were cast, and James Dean was voted the "Audie" for Best Actor (*East of Eden*). He received a posthumous standing ovation.

**A7**  **Best Actor** (1955). England's *Picturegoer* magazine named James Dean as Best Actor for his performance in *East of Eden*.

**A8**  **Best Actor** (1955). From the British Academy Awards, for *East of Eden*.

**A9**  **Best Foreign Actor** (1955). Dean received France's Crystal Star Award for his performance in *East of Eden*.

**A10**  **Best Actor** (1955). From the National Association of Theatre Owners, for *East of Eden*.

**A11**  **Golden Globe** (1955). James Dean received a special posthumous award from the Hollywood Foreign Press Association.

**A12**  **Special Achievement Silver Cup Award** (1955). On the November 27, 1955 episode of the *Colgate Comedy Hour*, *Modern Screen* magazine honored the late James Dean; "A gifted young actor was taken from us this year, but not before you recognized his genius and exciting potential. His name was Jimmy Dean and to him--in your name--we present the *Modern Screen* Special Achievement Award for 1955. No star deserved it more."

**A13**  **Photoplay  Gold Medal Special Achievement Award** (1955). Presented to Dean by the editors of *Photoplay* magazine for "his outstanding dramatic performances in *East of Eden* and *Rebel Without a Cause*." Wrote *Photoplay*, " his brilliant and tragically brief career can serve as his own monument. There it stands, to show other young actors how much can be accomplished in a short time if genuine ability is combined with intensity of purpose and a sincere feeling of dedication."

**A14   The Million Pearl Award** (1956). Dean received this Japanese award as Best Foreign Actor for *East of Eden*.

**A15   Academy Award nomination** (1956). James Dean received his second nomination for Best Actor for his performance as Jett Rink in *Giant*. He lost to Yul Brynner in *The King and I.*

**A16   Golden Globe** (1956). Dean was named the male "World Film Favorite" award.

**A17   Best Actor nomination** (1956). The New York Film Critics nominated Dean as Best Actor in *Giant*. He lost to Kirk Douglas in *Lust for Life*.

**A18   Best Male Star** (1956). Presented by Japan's Yokohama Movie Circle Council.

**A19   Top Foreign Actor** (1956). For his performance in *Rebel Without a Cause*, Dean received Top Foreign Actor honors from the Tokyo (Japan) Movie Fan's Association.

**A20   Best Performance by a Supporting Actor** (1956). Five actors were honored by *Film Daily* magazine for the supporting performances in 1956 films; James Dean (*Giant*), Anthony Perkins (*Friendly Persuasion*), Arthur O'Connell (*Picnic*), Rod Steiger (*The Court-Martial of Billy Mitchell*) and Oscar Homolka (*War and Peace*).

**A21   The Lawrence Hutton Hall of Fame** (1956). Memorials of "the immortals of art" are enshrined at the Lawrence Hutton Hall of Fame, located on the campus of Princeton University. A life mask of James Dean was added to the Hall in 1956, where it can be viewed alongside monuments to Edwin Booth, Ludwig von Beethoven, William Thackeray and John Keats. Dean is the youngest artist ever so honored.

**A22   Best Actor** (1957). Dean received France's Winged Victory

Award for his performance in *Giant*.

**A 23  Hollywood Walk of Fame** (1960). James Dean's star on the Walk of Fame is located at 1717 Vine Street.

**A 24  The James Dean Memorial Rod Run** (1961). In Fairmount, Indiana, James Dean fan Fred Stocker originated a car show that was held during the town's Museum Days Festival. Since 1961, the James Dean Memorial Rod Run has been an annual event. Only pre-1970 cars need apply.

**A 25  The James Dean Room** (1975). The Fairmount Historical Museum was founded in 1975. In its James Dean Room, which pays tribute to Fairmount's most famous citizen, visitors can see Dean's high school trophies, artwork and yearbooks, along with other assorted memoribilia.

**A 26  The James Dean Memorial** (1977). Japanese businessman Seita Ohnishi, one of the most celebrated James Dean fans, spent $50,000 to commission a stainless steel memorial to Dean, which was erected in front of the Cholame, California Post Office. The post office is located about a half-mile from the site where Dean was killed in 1955.

**A 27  The James Dean Memorial Run** (1978). Since 1978, James Dean fans with vintage automobiles have flocked to Los Angeles in the last weekend of September to participate in the James Dean Memorial Run. The rally begins in Van Nuys, and follows the route that Dean drove on the day of his death.

**A 28  A Tribute to James Dean** (January 24, 1983). The Academy of Motion Picture Arts and Sciences sponsored an evening of discussion, film clips, and a screening of *Rebel Without a Cause*. Among the guests in attendance at the academy's Samuel Goldwyn Theatre in Beverly Hills were Martin Landau, Bill Bast and Jim Backus.

**A 29  The James Dean Walking Tour of New York Hangouts** (1983). Every June since 1983, David Loehr, dubbed the "dean of Deanabilia" for his enormous collection of James Dean memoribilia, conducts a six-hour tour of Dean's favorite New York haunts.

**A30** **James Dean Day** (September 30, 1985). The thirtieth anniversary of James Dean's death was marked by articles in several newspapers and magazines, and on television. In Los Angeles, Mayor Tom Bradley declared September 30, 1985 to be "James Dean Day."

**A31** **Museum of Broadcasting Tribute** (February-March 1986). Separate tributes were held in New York at 1 East 53rd Street, and in Los Angeles at the Leo S. Bing Theatre, Los Angeles County Museum of Art. Highlights included screenings of Dean's early television appearances.

**A32** **The James Dean Gallery** (September 22,1988). David Loehr's collection of Dean memoribilia was put on permanent display in a twelve-room Victorian-style house at 425 Main Street, Fairmount, Indiana. Thousands of items, including costumes from Dean's films, photographs and a Warner Bros. life mask can be viewed for a $2 admission fee.

**A33** **Griffith Park Monument** (November 1,1988). The observatory in Los Angeles' Griffith Park became a part of motion picture history after its appearance in *Rebel Without a Cause*. On November 1, 1988, a bronze bust of James Dean created by Kenneth Kendall was dedicated on the observatory's front lawn.

# 9

# WHAT MIGHT HAVE BEEN

**W 1** *The Egyptian* (20th Century-Fox, 1954).

Marlon Brando turned down the role of Sinuhe in this would-be epic about a physician in pre-Christian times who has an affair with one of the Pharaoh's mistresses. After Brando's departure, James Dean was offered the role, but he likewise turned it down. Despite a prestigious cast (Peter Ustinov, Jean Simmons, Gene Tierney, Victor Mature), impressive sets and Michael Curtiz at the helm, the film was an epic disaster at the box office.

**W 2** *The Silver Chalice* (Warner Bros., 1954).

Paul Newman made his film debut as Basil the Defender, a role that James Dean rejected, in *The Silver Chalice*. The film is a fictional account of a sculptor (Newman) commissioned to create a receptacle for the chalice used by Jesus Christ at the Last Supper. The result was a critical and box office failure, and remains a source of embarrassment for its star.

**W 3** *Battle Cry* (Warner Bros., 1955).

An overlong adaptation of the Leon Uris novel that follows a battalion of soldiers from basic training to their first taste of action in New Zealand. James Dean auditioned for the role of Danny, but he lost out to Tab Hunter. Hunter was later considered for the role that Dean made legendary in *Rebel Without a Cause*.

**W 4** *The Battler* (NBC-TV, October 18, 1955).

Dean had filmed a promotional spot for this adaptation of Ernest

Hemmingway's short story, to be presented on *Pontiac Presents Playwrights 56*, just before his death. Production resumed afterward with Dewey Martin in the lead role of Nick Adams.

## W5 *The Cobweb* (MGM, 1955).

Dean was the first choice of producer John Houseman and director Vincente Minnelli to play Steven W. Holte, a patient in a psychiatric clinic. But Warner Bros. blocked the deal, and the role was given to John Kerr.

## W6 *Oklahoma!* (Magna Theatres, 1955).

Believe it or not, James Dean was at one time under consideration for the role of Curly, in Fred Zinnemann's outstanding adaptation of the classic Rodgers and Hammerstein musical. One can only wonder how his performance of "Oh, What a Beautiful Morning" would have compared to that of Gordon MacRae.

## W7 *Gun For a Coward* (??).

Warner Bros. purchased *Gun For a Coward*, a western, for James Dean, but after Dean's death the company abandoned the project, and the film was never made.

## W8 *The Corn is Green* (NBC-TV, January 18, 1956).

Dean was to star as Morgan Evans in this *Hallmark Hall of Fame* presentation opposite Judith Anderson. Anderson dropped out after Dean's death, and the program was broadcast with John Kerr and Eve La Gallienne as the stars.

## W9 *Somebody Up There Likes Me* (MGM, 1956)

Paul Newman, who made his film debut in one of Dean's rejects (see W2), became a star in this biopic of boxer Rocky Graziano. Prior to his death, Dean had agreed to play Graziano, and he was eager to display the boxing skills he had learned for *East of Eden*. Director Robert Wise chose Newman after Dean's death.

## W10 *Fear Strikes Out* (Paramount, 1957)

Paramount negotiated with Warner Bros. to obtain James Dean for its proposed adaptation of the autobiography of baseball player Jimmy

Piersall. Anthony Perkins played Piersall.

## W11  *The Spirit of St. Louis* (Warner Bros., 1957).

One would not expect James Dean and James Stewart, born twenty-three years apart, to contend for the same roles in Hollywood. However, Stewart campaigned for the role of Jett Rink in *Giant*, and after Dean turned down the chance to play Charles Lindbergh in *The Spirit of St. Louis*, it was Stewart who eventually stepped in.

## W12  *Damn Yankees* (Warner Bros., 1958).

Dean was considered for the role of Joe Hardy in George Abbott's film adaptation of the hit Broadway musical, but there is no evidence that he was ever offered the role. Tab Hunter played Hardy.

## W13  *The Left-Handed Gun* (Warner Bros., 1958).

*The Left-Handed Gun*, one of the most accurate cinematic portrayals of Billy the Kid, is perhaps the most intriguing of the projects that Dean expressed interest in before his death. For the third time, Paul Newman was the recipient of a role that Dean did not live to play.

## W14  *The Little Prince* (Paramount, 1974).

Antoine de Saint-Exupery's *The Little Prince* was one of James Dean's favorite books, and he had hoped to one day direct a film version. Nearly twenty years would pass before the material wound up on the big screen. Stanley Donen's musical treatment starred Richard Kiley, Steven Warner, Bob Fosse and Gene Wilder, with songs by Frederick Loewe and Alan Jay Lerner.

Director George Stevens advises James Dean on the set of Dean's last film, *Giant*, 1956. (Photograph courtesy of Photofest)

# 10

# TRIBUTES

## STAGE

**T-S1 DEAN** (London Casino, London, England August 30, 1977. 7 performances.)

### Credits
Directed by Robert H. Livingstone; Written by John Howlett; Produced by Steven Bentnick; Music by Robert Campbell; Scenery by Terry Parsons; Lighting by Nick Chelton; Choreography by Noel Tovey

### Cast
Glenn Conway (James Dean), Anna Nicholas (Pier Angeli) Murray Kash (Elia Kazan, Nicholas Ray, George Stevens), Peter Karrie, John Blythe, Jill Jarress, Betty Benfield, Marlene MacKay, Oscar James, Ken Caswell, Lesley Hand, Anthony O'Keeffe, Robert Booth, Alastair Kerr, Jane Egan, Marc Anthony, Beverley Elman, Matt Zimmerman, Dudley Rogers

### Synopsis
After gaining success on the Broadway stage in *The Immoralist*, James Dean departs for Hollywood and becomes a sensation overnight in *East of Eden*. Using memories of his bereaved childhood, Dean creates a mesmerizing portrait of alienated youth. The achievement of his goal is diminished by constant battles with Warner Bros., and a heartbreaking broken affair with actress Pier Angeli.

### Reviews
"(Glenn) Conway succeeds in building a coherent portrait of a man who is at once loyal and faithless, ignorant and extremely well-informed about his own profession, and capable of elaborate ironic courtesy as well as

coarse insult. Musically, the show contains some serviceable rock. . .(but there are no remarkable voices in the company." (*London Times*, August 31, 1977)

## Commentary
John Howlett, author of the book *James Dean: A Biography* (1975), collaborated with songwriter Robert Campbell to create a musical based on the life of James Dean. Glenn Conway, who played Dean, was lauded in reviews for his physical resemblance to the actor, and his recreation of Dean's slouch and mannerisms. The show was a flop, however, and closed after one week.

## T-S2 COME BACK TO THE 5 & DIME, JIMMY DEAN, JIMMY DEAN (Martin Beck Theatre, New York City, February 18, 1982.)

### Credits
Directed by Robert Altman; Written by Ed Graczyk; Produced by Dan Fisher, Joseph Clapsaddle, Joel Brykman and Jack Lawrence; Scenery by David Grapman; Costumes by Scott Bushnell; Lighting by Paul Gallo; Sound by Richard Fitzgerald

### Cast
Sudie Bond (Juanita), Cher (Sissy), Sandy Dennis (Mona), Mark Patton (Joe), Gena Ramsel (Sue Ellen), Kathy Bates (Stella May), Marta Heflin (Edna Louise), Ann Risley (Martha), Dianne Turley Travis (Alice Ann), Ruth Miller (Clarissa), Karen Black (Joanne)

### Synopsis
Five women from the same small town in Texas, best friends during their adolescence, reunite at their favorite former hangout, the town 5 & Dime store. All five recall crushes on James Dean, but one woman, Mona, still clings to the belief that she had an affair with the actor while he was in Marfa, Texas, shooting *Giant*, and that Dean is the father of her boy, Jimmy. Gradually, with the help of her friends, she shatters the self-generated illusion.

### Reviews
"Utterly preposterous and strangely unpleasant." (*New York Daily News*, February 19, 1982)

"There is a mixture of pompous simplicity and garbage-like symbolism about (the play) that is downright unappealing." (*New York Post*, February

19, 1982)

"Stripped of its endless repetitions, Jimmy Dean would shrink from two hours-plus to roughly eight minutes. The author's thematic obsession seems to be his heroines' sexual organs, which he variously reveals to be disfigured, malfunctioning or misplaced by evening's end. . . .Neither the gimmicky plot nor its cliched` participants are credible." (*New York Times*, February 19, 1982)

## Commentary
Robert Altman was at the helm and the cast contained three once and future Academy Award-winning actresses, but *Come Back to the 5 & Dime, Jimmy Dean, Jimmy Dean* was still on the receiving end of disastrous reviews. Most of the blame was leveled at Ed Graczyk's script, described in the *New York Times* as "shameless." The only beneficiary of the project is Cher, who launched her legitimate acting career with this play after replacing Shelley Duvall prior to the start of rehersals. *Jimmy Dean* was adapted into a film in 1982, with the same cast and director. Reviews were only slightly better, but the public again stayed away.

## T-S3 JAMES DEAN: A  DRESS REHERSAL (Regional
theatre, Denver, Colorado, 1984.)

## Commentary
Patricia Leone wrote and produced *James Dean: A  Dress Rehersal*, and opened the play in Denver with Stephen Brannan as Dean. Leone later tried without success to open the play off-Broadway, and it has not been staged since 1984.

## T-S4 MUSICAL SELECTIONS FROM REBEL: THE
JAMES DEAN MUSICAL (The Eighty-Eights Theater, New York City, May 15, 1989.)

## Commentary
*Musical Selections from Rebel* ran from May 15 to June 16, 1989, but was not reviewed and has yet to be revived. It is uncertain as to whether the proudction was meant as a precursor to a musical entitled *Rebel* that never materialized, or if the show opened in its completed form.

## T-S5 JAMES DEAN: THE NIGHT BEFORE (Kafe Kafka
Bistro Dinner Theatre, November 18, 1993.)

## Credits
Directed, written and produced by Dan Sefton

## Cast
Wil Hall (James Dean), Dan Sefton (Bob Smith)

## Synopsis
In the Villa Capri restaurant in Los Angeles, the night before James Dean's fatal car accident, Dean is interviewed by journalist Bob Smith.

## Reviews
"It's basic celebrity docudrama that might satisfy Dean fans." (*Los Angeles Times*, November 19, 1993)

"The talent is there, it just needs a better venue." (*Valley Life*, November 19, 1993)

# TELEVISION

## T-T1  JAMES DEAN REMEMBERED (ABC, 1974; 60 minutes; black and white and color)

## Credits
Directed by Jack Haley, Jr.; Written and produced by Al Ramrus; Coproduced by Ronald Lyon; Narrated by Peter Lawford

## Commentary
A diverse assortment of one-on-one interviews, conducted by Peter Lawford, with Sal Mineo, Sammy Davis, Jr., Natalie Wood, Steve Allen, and Leonard Rosenman.

## T-T2  JAMES DEAN (NBC, February 19, 1976; 99 minutes; color)

## Credits
Directed by Robert Butler; Written by Bill Bast; Produced by Bill Bast and John Forbes; Edited by John A. Martinelli; Music by Billy Goldenberg; Photographed by Frank Stanley

## Cast
Stephen McHattie (James Dean), Michael Brandon (Bill Bast), Candy Clark (Chris), Meg Foster (Dizzy), Jayne Meadows (Reva Randall), Dane Clark (James Whitmore), Katherine Helmond (Claire Folger), Heather Menzies (Jan), Amy Irving (Norma Jean), Brooke Adams (Beverly), Jack

Murdock (Judge), James O'Connell (Mr. Robbins), Leland Palmer (Arlene), Chris White (Secretary)

## Reviews

"*James Dean*. . .is a total entertainment wash-out. As a show business story, it's hokey and cliche bound. It also falls short as an examination of a mythic celebrity, offering specious insights and obvious irony. On a personal level, (Bill) Bast is cautious and oblique more often than not. What emerges is trite, boring and an absolute waste of time." (*New Orleans Times-Picayune*, February 19, 1976)

"*James Dean* may not have much new to tell us about its subject--but the two-hour film is better than most TV movies, and it does present an affecting study of a friendship bordering on love affair." (*Washington Post*, February 19, 1976)

## Commentary

Written and coproduced by Bill Bast, the man who was arguably James Dean's closest friend during the last five years of Dean's life, *James Dean* is a sincere, impressive made-for-TV movie that features an extraordinary performance by Stephen McHattie. In long and mid-shots, McHattie's resemblance to Dean is astonishing, and his voice contains enough of Dean's sandy, Indiana twang to make his portrayal even more convincing.

The film opens and closes with brief scenes of Bast in therapy, discussing his recollections of James Dean to a psychiatrist. The rest is flashback, beginning with Dean's first meeting with Bast at UCLA, and ending with the last time Bast saw Dean alive. To his credit, Bast writes mainly of those moments in Dean's life of which he has first-hand knowledge. As a result, *James Dean* is more a personal remembrance than a full-fledged biography, but its coverage of Dean's rise to stardom, and the conflicting feelings of admiration and envy experienced by his best friend, is insightful and often captivating.

## T-T3 FOREVER JAMES DEAN (Cinemax, 1988; 69 minutes; black and white and color)

## Credits

Directed, written and produced by Ara Chekmayan; Executive produced by Jeff Lawenda and Michael Yudin; Researched by David Loehr, Susan Bluttman and David Dalton; Song "American Rebel" composed by George Elworthy; Narrated by Bob Gunton

## Commentary

A reverent, '101' treatment of Dean's life, career and legacy, that mixes fact with a little bit of legend. The ponderous narration by Bob Gunton ("He played the congas. He raced cars. He was polite. He was angry.") detracts from the quality of the interviews with Bill Bast, Adeline Nall, Corey Allen, George Barris, Rex Bright, Jack Grinnage, Julie Harris, Kenneth Kendall, Beverly Long, Frank Mazzola, Bob Pulley, Bob Roth, Steffi Sidney, and Frank Worth. The highlight is some amusing screen test footage from *East of Eden* with Dean and Julie Harris.

## FILM

### T-F1 THE JAMES DEAN STORY (George Robert Productions, 1957; 80 minutes; black and white)

#### Credits
Directed by Robert Altman; Written by Stewart Stern; Produced by Robert Altman and George W. George; Music by Leith Stevens, song "Let Me Be Loved" by Jay Livingston and Ray Evans

#### Reviews
"It should be an effective contribution to the perpetuation of the James Dean myth." (*New York Times*, October 19, 1957)

"It is difficult to determine whether *The James Dean Story* is simply a shrewd exploitation piece or a sincere tribute from the company for which he worked. Perhaps it is a bit of both. (*Saturday Review*, August 3, 1957)

#### Commentary
Distributed by Warner Bros., as a tribute to the actor that constantly exasperated the studio while he worked there, *The James Dean Story* is the first documentary to explore Dean's life and legacy, and remains the most inept treatment of the subject to date.

Promotion of the film promised that James Dean "plays himself," through the use of existing motion picture material, tape recordings of his voice, and what is described as "dynamic exploration of the still photograph." Narrator Martin Gabel, in tones so grandiose that they border on self-parody, "interviews" several of Dean's friends and family members, including Marcus and Ortense Winslow and Lewis Bracker. Gabel's questions and the answers he received were awkwardly patched together in post-production, and as a result the interviewees seem stiff and mannered. At times, Ortense seems to read from a prepared script.

Stewart Stern, who wrote the film *Rebel Without a Cause*, has penned a script that amounts to nothing less than a deification of James Dean. "He looked at the ocean. . .and was jealous of its power. As an

actor he could be the ocean. . .and flood everything with his power,"
writes Stern, who when he's not being pretentious is being inaccurate;
Dean was not, as is stated here, a "model student" at UCLA.

Watching the results, it is not surprising to discover that members
of Dean's family only agreed to participate in the project after the
producers agreed to donate five percent of the net profits to the James
Dean Memorial Foundation. Sadly, that didn't amount to very much; the
film was released on August 13, 1957, and despite the still-prominent
hoopla surrounding Dean's tragic, premature death, *The James Dean
Story* was a colossal flop.

## T-F2 JAMES DEAN: THE FIRST AMERICAN
TEENAGER (Visual Programme Systems, Ltd.,1976, color
and black and white. 80 minutes)

### Credits
Directed and written by Ray Connolly; Produced by David Puttman and
Sandy Lieberson; Narrated by Stacy Keach

### Reviews
"While it certainly belongs in a Grade-B genre, the film provides insight
and interest in a  long-dead actor who has remained popular decades
after his death." (*Atlanta Journal*, November 23, 1976)

"The interviews are really, despite the visual grip of the Dean reels, the
substance of the film. They are artfully stitched into the fabric of the
visuals, selectively backgrounded and usually alive with the ring of
personal experience. . .this documentary revives for those old enough
the remarkable fascination and rebellious wellsprings that Dean
represented." (*Los Angeles Herald-Examiner*, June 9, 1976)

"If anything, the film excerpts. . .leave one to wonder what the fuss was
about. The aura has left the image, and only the pout remains." (*New York
Times*, October 19, 1976)

"All in all, it's compulsive stuff for the buff, neatly edited, written and
commented. What continues to amaze, as a lingering impression, is how
little the Dean material--and indeed image--has aged." (*Variety*, October
8, 1976)

### Commentary
One of the few documentaries to include actual footage from Dean's
three films and numerous television appearances, *James Dean: The First*

*American Teenager* is the best of the theatrically-released tributes. Joining such familiar interview subjects as Dennis Hopper, Sal Mineo, Natalie Wood, Corey Allen, Christine White, Nicholas Ray and Leonard Rosenman, are some interesting new faces, including actress Leslie Caron and Gene Owen, who was Dean's drama teacher at Santa Monica City College.

## T-F3 SEPTEMBER 30, 1955 (Universal, 1977; 101 minutes; color)

### Credits
Directed and written by James Bridges; Produced by Jerry Weintraub; Photographed by Gordon Willis (Technicolor); Music by Leonard Rosenman; Edited by Jeff Gourson; Art direction by Robert Luthardt; Set direction by Sharon Thomas; Costumes by Kent Warner, Patricia Zinn and Mina Mittleman; Stunts by R. A. Rondell

### Cast
Richard Thomas (Jimmy J.), Susan Tyrrell (Melba Lou), Deborah Benson (Charlotte), Lisa Blount (Billie Jean), Thomas Hulce (Hanley), Dennis Quaid (Frank), Mary Kai Clark (Pat), Dennis Christopher (Eugene), Collin Wilcox (Jimmy J's Mother), Ben Fuhrman (Coach), Ouida White (Aunt Ethel ), Bryan Scott (Dickie), Glen Irby (Band Director), Mike Farris (Edgar), Tom Bonner (Radio Announcer), Bush Satterfield (Charlotte's Father), Katherine Satterfield (Charlotte's Mother), Betty Harford (Nurse), James Dombek (Mr. Brown), Belynda Dix (Girl in Car), Melody Hamilton (Girl with Corsage), Ray Hemphill (Young Man in Truck), Tex Biggs (Old Man in Truck), John Pearce (TV Man), Peter Boggs (Mr. Phillips), Mark Thomas, Paula Sanford, Freeman Mobley, Charles McCrary, George Johnson, Neal Moore, Mark Andrews, Ron Campbell, Brian Brandt

### Synopsis
On September 30, 1955, teenagers Jimmy J. and Billie Jean are devastated to learn that their idol, James Dean, has perished. Together with several friends, they stage a seance-like ceremony to honor Dean. After the participants become drunk, the ceremony takes a violent turn, and Billie Jean's face is disfigured.

### Reviews
"It is beautifully cast and acted with self-absorbed intensity by a number of young performers who are very, very funny." (*New York Times*, March 31, 1978)

"An excellent film." (*Variety*, August 31,1977)

## Commentary
Writer/director James Bridges, whose film *The Paper Chase* was a surprise hit in 1973, based *September 30, 1955* on his own idolization of James Dean, and on a play he had previously written entitled *How Many Times Did You See East of Eden?*. The film was well-reviewed by the few critics who saw it, but was not a popular success.

## T-F4 COME BACK TO THE 5 & DIME, JIMMY DEAN, JIMMY DEAN (Viacom, 1982; 109 minutes; color)

### Credits
Directed by Robert Altman; Written by Ed Graczyck, based on his play; Produced by Scott Bushnell; Photographed by Pierre Mignot; Edited by Jason Rosenfield; Production designed by David Gropman

### Cast
Sandy Dennis (Mona), Cher (Sissy), Karen Black (Joanne), Sudie Bond (Juanita), Marta Heflin (Edna Louise), Kathy Bates (Stella May), Mark Patton (Joe Qualley), Caroline Aaron (Martha), Ruth Miller (Clarissa), Gena Ramsel (Sue Ellen), Ann Risley (Phyllis Marie), Dianne Turley Travis (Alice Ann)

### Reviews
"There are some interesting things about Robert Altman's (film), but they have less to do with anything on the screen than with the manner in which the film was produced and with Mr. Altman's unflagging if misguided faith in the project." (*New York Times*, October 12, 1982)

### Commentary
*Come Back to the 5 & Dime, Jimmy Dean, Jimmy Dean* is a faithful adaptation of the the 1982 play, with the same cast and director.

## VIDEOCASSETTE

## T-V1 HOLLYWOOD: THE REBELS--JAMES DEAN
(CIAK Studio, 1985; 90 minutes; color and black and white)

### Credits
Directed by Claudio Masenza; Produced by Donatella Baglivo; Music by Flavio Emilio Scogna

### Commentary
In the mid-1970s, Italy's CIAK Studios released a series of three

documentaries on James Dean, Marlon Brando and Montgomery Clift, under the title *Hollywood: The Rebels*. The Dean film is a superb treatment, in which director Claudio Masenza strikes an ideal balance between interviews, film clips and archival footage. Producer Donatella Baglivo wisely opted to proceed without a narrator, and instead allow the story to be told entirely through the recollections of Dean's friends and coworkers, including Martin Landau, Bill Bast, Bill Gunn, Christine White, Dizzy Sheridan, Julie Harris, Dennis Hopper, Roy Schatt and Corey Allen. Highlights include the Pepsi commercial that was Dean's first on-camera job, *East of Eden* screen test footage featuring Dean and Richard Davalos, clips from the television dramas *Hill Number One* and *The Unlighted Road*, and an interview with Ruth Goetz, coauthor of *The Immoralist*. "He was the most exasperating young actor I've ever worked with," recalls Goetz of her days on Broadway with Dean; "He was wonderful onstage, and detestable backstage."

## T-V2 BYE BYE JIMMY (1990, 60 minutes, color and black and white)

**Credits**
Directed and produced by Nick Taylor and Paul Watson; Narrated by Nick Clemente

**Commentary**
This British documentary, never aired in the United States, follows a collection of vintage cars through the last road taken by Dean. Music provided by Jerry Lee Lewis, the Beach Boys and Buddy Holly is interspersed with interviews.

# MUSIC

## T-M1 THE JAMES DEAN STORY (1956, Coral Records 57099)

This tribute album, narrated by Steve Allen and Bill Randle, mixes music and dialogue from *East of Eden* and *Rebel Without a Cause*, with original songs performed by Dick Jacobs, Jimmy Wakely and George Cates. Songs include "Jimmy, Jimmy," "His Name Was Dean," "We'll Never Forget You," "James Dean (Just a Boy from Indiana)," "There's Never Been Anyone Else But You," and "The Ballad of James Dean."

## T-M2 THE JAMES DEAN STORY (1957, Capitol Records W881)

Soundtrack album, featuring music composed by Leith Stevens, from the documentary *The James Dean Story* (see T-F1).

## T-M3 SEPTEMBER 30, 1955 (1977, MCA Records 2313)

Soundtrack from the film (see T-F3), featuring music by Leonard Rosenman, performed by the Leonard Rosenman Orchestra.

## T-M4 JAMES DEAN: HE NEVER SAID GOODBYE
### (Caprice Records)

Rod Wimmer, a singer/songwriter from Indiana, wrote and recorded this tribute album to Dean, which includes the songs "He Never Said Goodbye," "Go Back With Me," "The Gift," "Momma's Hope, Momma's Dream," "Love I Believed Your Lie," "Because of My Dreams," "That Tree Upon the Hill," "Where I'll Never Say Goodbye to You," "I'd Like to be Alone With You," and "I'm Just the Singer of the Song."

## T-M5 MUSIC JAMES DEAN LIVED BY (Unique Records)

The themes from *East of Eden*, *Rebel Without a Cause* and *Giant* are performed here by Joe Leahy's Orchestra and Chorus. Vocalists Jack Carroll and Bob Graybo contribute original songs, including "The Story of James Dean," "I'll Close My Eyes," "Misunderstood," "Give Me a Moment Please," Dream Lover," "Masquerade," and "We Could Make Such Beautiful Music Together."

## T-M6 THEME MUSIC FROM THE JAMES DEAN STORY (World Pacific Records)

Famed jazz musician Chet Baker, accompanied by Bud Shank, performs Leonard Rosenman's music from 1957's *The James Dean Story*.

## T-M7 A TRIBUTE TO JAMES DEAN (Columbia Records)

Music from *East of Eden*, *Rebel Without a Cause* and *Giant*, performed by Ray Heindorf and the Warner Bros. Orchestra.

## T-M8 A TRIBUTE TO JAMES DEAN (MGM Records)

Art Mooney performs music from James Dean's three motion pictures.

## T-M9 A TRIBUTE TO JAMES DEAN (Imperial Records 9021)

Similar to T-M7 and T-M8, with composer Leonard Rosenman conducting.

### SONGS INSPIRED BY JAMES DEAN

| | |
|---|---|
| "The Ballad of James Dean" | Dick Jacobs |
| "The Ballad of James Dean" | The Four Tunes |
| "Come Back Jimmy Dean, Jimmy Dean | Bette Midler |
| "Deanie Boy" | Tommy Deans Orchestra |
| "Dean's 11th Dream" | James Dean Driving Experience |
| "He's My Jim" | Joanna Dean |
| "His Name Was Dean" | Don Sargeant |
| "Home in Indiana, James Dean" | Red River Dave |
| "I Miss You Jimmy" | Veretta Dillard |
| "James Dean" | The Eagles |
| "James Dean" | The Goo Goo Dolls |
| "James Dean" | The Jets |
| "James Dean" | The Kevin Brown Band |
| "Jamie Boy" | Kay Starr |
| "Jim Dean of Indiana" | Phil Ochs |
| "Jimmy, Jimmy" | Madonna |
| "Let Me Be Loved" | Eydie Gorme |
| "Ridin' With James Dean" | Joan Jett |
| "A Young Man Is Gone" | The Beach Boys |

# INDEX

This index refers to page numbers as well as to entry codes in enumerated sections. Entries preceded by "A" can be found under Awards, by "B" in the Bibliography, by "D" in the Discography, by "F" in the Filmography, by "R" under Radio, by "S" under Stage Work, by "T" in Televison, by "W" under "What Might Have Been," and by "T-(F,M,S,T,V) under Tributes. For page numbers of the coded chapters, refer to the table of contents.

Bean, Robin, B088
Beata, Abby, B089
Beath, Warren Newton, B010
*Big Story, The*, T18
*Biographical Dictionary of Film, The*, B068
*Blackboard Jungle, The*, F5
*Blessings in Disguise*, B034
Bluttman, Susan, B091
Bogart, Humphrey, 1,F4
Boller, Paul F., B011
Borgnine, Ernest, 18,F4
Bosworth, Patricia, B012
*Boulevard of Broken Dreams: The Life, Times and Legend of James Dean*, B003
Brackett, Rogers, 6,8,9,S6,F1,F3,R1
Brando, Marlon, 13,F4,F5,F6,B013
*Brando: The Unauthorized Biography*, B037
Brannan, Stephen, T-S3
Brean, Joel, B014
Bridges, James, T-F3
Browne, David, B092
Brynner, Yul, 18
Burns, Keith, B002
Burr, Ty, B093
Burton, Richard, F6
*Bye Bye Jimmy*, T-V2

Cameron, Victor V. (Dr.), 2
Campbell, Robert, T-S1
*Campbell Soundstage*, T15,T21
Capen, Jeanne Balch, B095
Capote, Truman, F4
Carey, Gary, B015
Carradine, John, 8
Carter, Lynne, B096,B097
Chastain, Sue, B099
Cher, T-S2
Christon, Lawrence, B100
Christopher, Wendy, B101

Clemens, Harry, B102
Clement, Hal, B103
Clift, Montgomery, 1,F6
Coburn, Charles, F3
*Cobweb, The*, W5
*Colgate Comedy Hour, The*, T34
Collins, Joan, B016
*Come Back to the 5 & Dime, Jimmy Dean, Jimmy Dean*, (film), T-F4
*Come Back to the 5 & Dime, Jimmy Dean, Jimmy Dean* (stage), T-S2
Connolly, Mike, B104
*Continuity and Evolution in a Public Symbol: An Investigation Into the Creation and Communication of the James Dean Image in Mid-Century America*, B069
*Conversations With Capote*, B033
Conway, Glenn, T-S1
Cooper, Dennis, B105
Corley, Ed, B017
Corman, Roger, F5
*Corn is Green, The*, W8
Covert, Colin, B107
Cronkite, Walter, T10
Cronyn, Hume, 8,B018
Cunningham, Terry, B019
*Current Affair, A*, T43,T44
Curtis Management Group, 19

Dalton, David, 7,B109,B020,B021
Damone, Vic, 12-13
*Damn Yankees*, W12
*Danger*, T12,T17,T25,T27
Davalos, Dick, 12,F4
Davidson, Sara, B043
Davis, Joan, 6
Davis, Ronald L., B011
Davis, Sammy Jr., B022
Dawber, Martin, B023
Deacy, Jane, 9,10,11,F6
Dean, Charlie, (uncle), 3
Dean, Emma (grandmother), 2,3

**About the Author**

DAVID HOFSTEDE is a free-lance writer. His previous books include *Audrey Hepburn: A Bio-Bibliography* (Greenwood Press, 1994).

.